# Hearing the

# Voice of the Customer

**Bill Inmon**

Tech    Publications

D1376729

Published by:

2 Lindsley Road

Basking Ridge, NJ 07920 USA

https://www.TechnicsPub.com

Edited by Sadie Hoberman

First Printing 2018

Copyright © 2018 by Bill Inmon

| | |
|---|---|
| ISBN, print ed. | 9781634623315 |
| ISBN, Kindle ed. | 9781634623322 |
| ISBN, ePub ed. | 9781634623339 |

Library of Congress Control Number: 2017964493

*For Patty Haines, who has been a good friend for as long as I can remember.*

# Contents

# Introduction

One hundred years ago, the voice of the customer was easily and routinely heard by the shopkeeper. In small towns, the shopkeeper knew everyone. The relationship between the shopkeeper and the customer was long standing and personal. The shopkeeper and the customer were neighbors and had probably gone to the same school together. They lived in the same small town and their children played together. They both rooted for their high school football team on autumn Friday nights. So when the customer walked into the shop, the shopkeeper immediately knows who they were.

Today's world has gotten much bigger and much more complex. No longer does the store owner personally know everyone who comes into the store. The store is too big, the population is too big and mobile for the same kind of personal relationship with the customer to exist as it once did, and there are lots more people in today's world. It is simply impossible for the shopkeeper to personally know every customer who walks in the door. And in today's world, the shop may well be a virtual shop—not a small store front on Main Street but a store on the Internet.

With growth, the march of time, and a changing marketplace, have come advances in technology. There are new technologies today that did not exist in a previous day and age.

It is still as important as it ever was for the store owner to listen to what the customer is saying. But the store owner listens far differently than he/she did a hundred years ago. In particular, there are three important technologies that make it possible to hear and listen to the voice of the customer today:

- The ability to acquire, store, and manage huge amounts of data

- The ability to read and understand text in a computerized environment

- The ability to visualize data so that management can comprehend what is being said by a database

While it is generally recognized by business that it is a good idea to listen to the customer, it is not clear as to how to go about listening to the customer. For all the advances in technology there are still formidable technological and economic challenges. So where is the voice of the customer heard today? The voice of the customer is heard in many places – on paper, on the Internet, through email, in call centers, in warranty claims, over the telephone and in many other places. In today's world the corporation needs to be able to listen to the customer in all of those places.

This book is a primer on how to go about hearing and listening to the voice of the customer using the technologies that are available today. This book answers important questions such as:

- Where is the voice of the customer heard?

- How does the corporation find and capture the voice of the customer?

- How is the voice of the customer actually interpreted and understood?

- How do you cope with the volume of messages the customer is sending you?

- How do you separate noise from the important messages?

- How do you analyze the composite voice of the customer over thousands of customers?

- How do you reduce the voice of the customer to a visual format that is understood by management?

- How do you know when the message the customer is sending changes?

After reading this book the reader will be able to manage, build, and operate a corporate infrastructure that listens to the voice of the customer.

This book is primarily for the business person—the top manager and the marketing manager. Others that will find this book of value are the sales manager, the finance manager, and other individuals making decisions in the corporation. In addition, the technician and the manager of technology will find this book of value.

This book belongs on the desk of every manager in the corporation who cares about:

- Increasing the revenue of the corporation

- Increasing and holding the market share of the corporation

- Reducing the expenses of the corporation.

As a quick anecdote, several years ago I was invited to speak to the CEO, CIO, and CFO of one of America's largest retailing corporations. I was given 30 minutes to speak. I was told that I was to talk about business, not technology. I carefully prepared my presentation.

I spoke on three subjects—increasing revenue, expanding your market share, and reducing expenses. At the end of my short presentation, the CEO thanked me for my presentation and said, "Thanks for the presentation, but our corporation just isn't interested in those kinds of things."

I came home and asked my wife if we had any stock in the corporation. If we did we needed to sell the stock immediately. It is a good thing because that very large retailer is today going out of business. (This is a true story!)

Of all the critical things a prosperous corporation needs to do, listening to the voice of the customer is at the very top of the list.

There are two ways the voice of the customer is heard: collectively and individually. Collectively, all of the customers of the corporation are heard. Management makes strategic decisions based on the collective voice of the customer. But the voice of the customer can be heard individually as well. On a call by call, interaction by interaction basis, the customer has a conversation with the company. In this case, decisions are made individually but not strategically. The voice of the customer is important in both cases. This book however is about the collective voice of the customer.

So if you are a business person and are interested in increasing revenue and market share and reducing expenses, then this book is for you.

The primary audience for this book is the business person. Having stated that, there are several places where the book takes a technical turn. In today's business world, the business person who turns his/her back on technology is an anachronism. The marketplace and the future of business are inexorably intertwined with technology. So it is time the businessperson starts to embrace technology.

I have attempted to keep the intrusions of technology in check. I have introduced discussions of technology only when necessary and I have tried to keep discussions of technology at a high comprehensible level.

If a person is going to understand the voice of the customer in today's world, a person is going to have to understand a little bit about technology, because that is where the voice of the customer is heard today.

No apologies.

*WHI, Castle Rock, CO February 2018*

# 1: Value

When I was in college, we used to drive to neighboring campuses for parties and mixers. On the way home, it was a tradition that late at night we would stop by Howard Johnson's. The orange roof was always a recognizable sight. But where is Howard Johnson's today? For that matter, where is the airline Pan Am? Or TWA? Or Woolworth's? Try finding a Bennigan's. Or a Hofbrau House.

There is a long line of businesses that once were household names that no longer exist today. Restaurants. Airlines. Retailers. Manufacturers. Every kind of business imaginable.

There are many reasons why businesses go under: changing market conditions, changing tastes, changing technology—but behind every reason is a basic and fundamental failing of businesses that go under. That failing is that businesses that fail **have not listened to their customer.**

When a business listens to and hears the voice of their customer, they are able to respond to their marketplace. When businesses do not listen to their customer they wake up one day to find that the world has passed them by. And when the world has passed a business by, the best that a business can do is to place themselves in a reactive, catch up mode. And when a business is in a reactive mode, making a profit and making new customers is hard to do.

Far and away, the businesses that are in a proactive mode are the businesses that find they have expanding revenues, an expanding customer base, and new opportunities. It is a tautology that businesses all strive to become and stay proactive. And the number one way that businesses become proactive is to hear and heed the voice of their customer.

Once upon a time, listening to the voice of the customer was easy to do. The customer was a neighbor who you knew from school, parties, and sports. Your children played with and went to school with your customer's children. So when your customer walked into your shop to make a purchase, you knew your customer. You knew the voice of your customer before he/she even spoke.

That was yesterday.

Today conditions are very different. Instead of one shop there are chains of shops in many different cities. There are shops on the Internet. Instead of a few people there are lots of people. And people are moving around all the time. People change jobs. People go off to school. People join the service. People are transferred to new locations.

It is impossible for today's shopkeeper to actually know the vast majority of people that come in and out of the shop today.

That is today.

Yet it is every bit as important to hear the voice of your customer today as it was yesterday. Perhaps even more important. What has changed is not the importance of hearing the voice of your customer, but *how* you hear the voice of your customer today.

If you want to stay in business, you *must* listen to the voice of your customer. There are a thousand good reasons to hear the voice of the customer. Some of those reasons include:

- Fostering repeat business. It is much easier to sell an existing customer than it is to make a new customer

- Becoming aware of changing market tastes and conditions

- Preserving market share

- Protecting and enhancing the public image of the corporation

The problem is that for all the value in hearing the voice of the customer, and for all the advancements made in technology, it is still hard to hear the voice of the customer. There are still plenty of obstacles to sensitizing the corporation to what the customer is trying to say.

## WHERE IS THE VOICE OF THE CUSTOMER?

So where is the voice of the customer heard today? In the crudest and most basic sense, the voice of the customer is heard when the customer makes a purchase. Simply measuring sales over time will tell the corporation what the customer is saying. But waiting for the customer to signal his/her intentions through measuring a change in buying patterns is a really crude and ineffective way to hear what the customer is saying. By the time the customer has changed buying patterns, it is too late to influence the customer.

In order to be effective, it is necessary to listen to the customer *before* their buying patterns have changed. The appropriate time to listen to the customer is at the moment when the buying patterns are in a state of flux, not after the patterns have changed.

So is it even possible to listen to the customer before buying patterns have changed? The answer is yes, of course it is possible.

Where then can the voice of the customer be heard while the customer is still deciding on how to make purchases?

There are many places where the voice of the customer can be heard:

- Emails
- Social media
- Over the Internet
- Call centers
- Help desks
- Warranty claims
- Insurance claims
- Scheduling dispatching

In short, wherever the customer has contact with the corporation is where it is possible to hear what the customer is saying. In the worst of cases, it is possible to at least be sensitive to the customer's intentions. In the best of cases it is possible to gain deep insights into what the customer has on his/her mind.

## WHAT IS THE CUSTOMER SAYING?

The corporation is interested in at least the following kinds of things the customer has to say:

- **Negative/positive comments on products and services.** How can the corporation improve? What is the corporation doing wrong? What especially pleases the customer? All of these thoughts should be known at every level of management.

- **Questions**. How does a product work? What should the product be doing? What speeds and capacities and limits does the product have? How is a product installed?

- **Warranties/guarantees**. How long is the warranty? What are the limits of the warranty? What is and is not covered by the warranty? What are the expiration terms of the warranty?

- **Complaints**. What was wrong with products and/or services? What remedies does the customer have? How can the malfunctions of the product/service be made whole or rectified to the customer?

- **Support**. What are the customer's expectations? What has been supplied by the corporation? Have those expectations been met? Are there legal obligations?

- **Want to purchase**. Does the customer want to buy a product or service? The customer wants to know what products and services are available and how much they cost. The customer has suggestions for new or enhanced products and services.

- **Availability**. What products and services are available? How much do they cost? Are there any prerequisites to purchase? What purchase options are available?

- **Service**. What are the service expectations? The customer wants to make logistics arrangements for having services done. How has the company failed to live up to the service expectations of the customer?

- **Compliments**. The customer wants to acknowledge exceptional service by an individual or a service unit. The customer wants to express delight at a product or service.

- **Surveys**. The customer makes his/her wishes or feelings known by means of a survey.

And this is just the short list of ways the customer expresses his/her attitudes and feelings. And the corporation ought to be especially sensitive and keen to listen to what the customer is saying. If the corporation is not listening, then the customer will find a corporation that is listening. At the very least, the customer will switch brands and loyalties to another corporation in the hopes that the new corporation will listen to the customer.

Stated differently:

> *The smartest thing a corporation can do is to listen to and respond to the voice of the customer.*

At an individual level, listening to the customer results in the sale and satisfaction of at least one unit of product or service. At a macro level, listening to the customer results in an increase and expansion of market share and an expansion of revenue.

## NEW CUSTOMERS VERSUS EXISTING CUSTOMERS

At the heart of listening to and responding to your customer is the fact the reselling to an existing customer is much easier than enticing a new customer. Once you have reduced the cost of a sale, you can then redirect capital to other parts of the corporation. In such a fashion the corporation grows and prospers.

## CHANGING MARKETPLACE

As important as reducing the cost of sales over time is, there are some other equally important reasons for listening to your customers. One of those reasons is that the marketplace changes all the time. Sometimes the changes are slow. Other times the changes are fast. But it is an immutable fact that over time changes will occur.

There are a thousand reasons for the ever changing marketplace. Some of the reasons are:

- **Competition**. There are new competitors or reenergized competitors in the marketplace

- **Technology**. There are new technological innovations every day

- **Economics.** The economics affecting a marketplace are in a constant state of evolution

- **Advent of new products.** New products are appearing all the time

- **Demographics of the marketplace.** The marketplace – its people, its corporations – all age one day at a time

- **Governing laws.** The laws that govern countries change over time

And there are probably plenty more reasons why a marketplace is in a constant state of upheaval.

And as the marketplace changes, its customers, the tastes of the customer, and the spending habits of the customer also change. A corporation that is aware of those changes is a corporation that is able to position themselves in a proactive state. If a corporation is unaware or unable to become aware of the changes in the marketplace, the corporation is automatically placed in a reactive state. And the difference between a corporation being proactive and reactive is the difference between being able to go on the offensive versus having to constantly be on the defensive.

Listening to the voice of the customer is at the heart of the proactivity or reactivity of the corporation in the marketplace.

There should be then no argument that listening to the voice of the customer is extremely important for every corporation to do and to do continuously.

## HOW TO LISTEN TO THE VOICE OF THE CUSTOMER?

For all of the advances made in technology, it would seem that finding and listening to the voice of the customer should be simple. But instead there are all sorts of obstacles to the challenge of finding and listening to the voice of the customer.

There are three big challenges to finding the voice of the customer:

- Finding and capturing the voice of the customer
- Transforming the voice of the customer
- Visualizing the voice of the customer

### FINDING THE VOICE OF THE CUSTOMER

The voice of the customer can be found in many places, such as on the Internet, in call centers, in help desks, and in customer surveys. Other places that the voice of the customer can be found are in warranties, insurance claims, and service requests. In some cases the voice of the customer is in a raw state—on paper or on a recording. When the voice of the customer is in a raw state, it must be transcribed into an electronic state. In other cases, the voice of the customer is in an electronic state and needs no transcription.

There is a phenomenon that must be factored in when looking at all these places. That phenomenon is that in most cases the voice of the customer is heard only when there has been a problem. Customers are motivated to issue a complaint only when there has been a problem. As long as the product or service has been satisfactory and meets the customer's expectations, there is no feedback. It is only when there has been a problem that the customer raises his/her voice. So it can be misleading to look at the feedback that the corporation gets because it is entirely possible that the vast majority of the customers are pleased or satisfied. The corporation only hears about the exceptions.

As a rule of thumb, one corporation believes that the ratio of positive comments to negative comments should be about 10% to 90%. In other words the corporation expects 90% of the feedback received by the corporation to be negative and 10% of the feedback to be positive. If the ratios significantly differ from this, the corporation knows that something is off base.

Another issue relating to the feedback of the voice of the customer is that of the privacy of the feedback. If the feedback is found on the Internet, then there is no privacy associated with the feedback. But if the feedback is derived privately, then the feedback becomes private property that needs to be protected and secured.

## TRANSFORMING THE VOICE OF THE CUSTOMER

Once the voice of the customer has been found, if transcription is necessary, the next step is to transform/transcribe the voice of the customer into an electronic form that can be analyzed. If no transcription is necessary, the voice of the customer is already in an electronic form.

It is a temptation to say that once the voice of the customer is in the form of electronic text, that text can be simply placed in a computer and the text can be analyzed. This, however, is a simplistic and naïve perspective. There are many reasons why just placing text inside a computer is not a foundation for analysis.

There are many problems with text. Some of the obvious problems with text are misspellings, transcription errors, and the need for cursory editing. But there is a much more serious, much more profound problem with just looking at electronic text. The problem is that in order to make sense of text you must also have the context of text. Text without context is meaningless. If you are going to understand and analyze text, you must have the context as well.

The problem with context is that usually context lies well outside the text itself. You simply cannot look at text and magically understand what the context is. Context often comes from many places well outside the conversation. Context may come from many places such as:

- The location the conversation is taking place in

- The age of the participants in the conversations

- The sex of the participants in the conversations

- The time of year the conversation is occurring

- The building the conversation is taking place in

- The state of mind of the participants in the conversations

- The time of day the conversation is taking place in

- Whether the participants in the conversation are at work

There are many, many factors that influence the context of a conversation. This list represents merely some of the obvious factors.

Another factor in the transformation of the voice of the customer into a form that can be analyzed is in dealing with volumes of data. It is one thing for the human mind to try to absorb text. It is another thing altogether for a computer to try to absorb a large volume of data. The human mind simply has finite limitations that are far below that of the computer.

For example, suppose that a person tries to read and understand the feedback from 40,000 customers. The person will be lucky to actually remember 10 comments after reading 40,000 comments. But a computer will remember and process all 40,000 comments.

There are other significant challenges to transforming the voice of the customer into a form that can be analyzed. But understanding the context of text and dealing with the volume of text that is encountered are the two largest issues.

## VISUALIZING THE VOICE OF THE CUSTOMER

After the voice of the customer has been transformed into a form that can be analyzed, the output of the transformation needs to be visualized. Management does not do well with data in the form of a database. Instead, management requires that data be transformed into the form of a visualization.

When data is visualized, management can look at:

- Summaries of numbers
- Trends over time
- Classifications of numbers
- Exceptions
- Contrasts of classifications of data

And management can look at these facts in a concise visual format. Management around the world prefers to see things in a visual format. And the voice of the customer is no different from other data. The third major challenge of hearing the voice of the customer is that the voice of the customer must be converted to a visual format.

## FEEDBACK TO THE CUSTOMER

Once the voice of the customer is heard, the next step is to provide feedback to the customer, to let the customer know that he/she has been heard. In some cases, the feedback is provided in a direct fashion. In other cases, the feedback is provided indirectly. And in the worst case no feedback at all is provided.

It is significant to note that even if no changes to the corporation are made or even going to be made, it is always pleasing to the customer to at least know that the voice of the customer has been recognized and heard.

## IN SUMMARY

Organizations that wish to stay in business *must* listen to the voice of the customer. Listening to the voice of the customer places the organization into a proactive position.

There are three major challenges in the listening to the voice of the customer:

- Capturing the voice of the customer and managing the volumes of data that ensue

- Converting the text into a form that can be analyzed by the computer

- Converting the text and analysis into a visualized format.

Inherent to the analysis of the voice of the customer is the understanding that often customers only raise their voice when there has been a problem. In addition, merely analyzing text is the first step to understanding the customer. Context of text is as important as the text itself.

# 2: Source

There are two places where the voice of the customer can be heard. Some text that represents the voice of the customer is public domain data such as from the Internet. When people put their comments out in public to be heard, anyone can read their comments and anyone can do whatever they wish with those comments. By placing comments in public, the author of the comments loses all rights to privacy. Certainly reading and analyzing those comments is fair use of the text.

The other place where the voice of the customer is heard is in internal documents. There are many forms of internal documents such as email, letters, memos, and surveys. Internal documents have the full protection and privacy of the corporation.

There are many places where the voice of the customer can be heard. Some of these places require their own technology in order to turn the text into a form that can be analyzed. When a technology is required to access the comments, those access technologies themselves have their own set of considerations.

Although the source of the voice of the customer arrives at the door step of the corporation in many fashions, it always boils down to being able to interpret and analyze text.

Fig 2.1 shows that the voice of the customer however it arrives, must be transformed into electronic text. Once the transformation into text is made, the text is then read into textual disambiguation. From textual disambiguation, text is transformed into records or occurrences of data where it can then be analyzed.

Figure 2.1 The voice of the customer ultimately ends up as text

## ON PAPER

The sentiment of the customer is often made, captured, and then printed out on paper. It is common for many organizations to use paper and to continue to use paper as the media on which the voice of the customer is transformed.

The problem with paper is that in order for paper to be used in analysis, the words on the paper must be captured and transformed into electronic text. Stated differently, the words on the paper must be transformed into an electronic format in order for the computer to be able to analyze the information.

There are two basic modes that paper-based document images can be captured: in a simple image (or snapshot) mode and in an electronic cognizant mode.

In the simple image snapshot mode, the document is captured but the words are still unknown to the computer. The words can be read by a human but the computer has no awareness of the words. A simple paper-based document image is like a Polaroid snapshot. The words are there but they are not electronically recognized as words by the computer.

The second mode in which a document can be captured and transformed into is the mode in which the words are electronically cognizant. This mode is usually called the "optical character recognition" or "OCR" mode.

OCR technology has been around for a long time and is a well-established technology. Fig 2.2 depicts the OCR mode of reading documents and lifting the text from the document.

Figure 2.2 Optical character recognition

There are many issues with OCR such as the technology, the cost, and the support from the vendor. But ultimately the important issues of OCR technology boil down to one subject: quality. Quality in the world of OCR technology refers to the accuracy with which the text is captured and understood. When OCR operates properly, the string of text "she rode in her Toyota, and felt very safe" is read and understood. But where OCR is defective, the string might appear as "&ne r0d3 1m n3r T0t0lq and k3iy u3rt 5ab3." The string that has been read has been interpreted into gibberish and cannot be meaningfully processed by the computer.

It is reasonable to expect OCR under optimal circumstances to achieve a 90% + level of accuracy. It is not reasonable to expect 100% accuracy of OCR in even the best of circumstances due to three factors:

- **Strike**. If the document has been printed with sufficient toner, the result should be very legible words. But if the toner is low or of poor quality, the strength of the ink on the paper may be weak. This makes it hard to read for OCR.

- **Font type**. There are many font types. If the font that has been used to print the document is a standard type, then that makes the text more readable for OCR. But if the font is not of a standard type (and most aren't) then the font type makes the text as presented on paper less than legible to OCR.

- **Paper.** If the paper is not smooth, clean, and white, the paper itself can conspire to make the printing less than legible to OCR.

These three factors all affect the quality of the end result of OCR processing.

## VOICE RECOGNITION

A second very common way the voice of the customer is heard is through voice recognition. Voice recognition is used in call centers, help desks, customer support, and other ways. In voice recognition, the transcript of the conversation that occurs is made. Then the recording of the transcript is turned into an electronic record of the conversation. Typical voice transcription is from a .wav format into a .txt format.

There is one major difference between OCR processing and voice recognition transcription. When people write they usually write in a fairly formal manner. But when people talk, usually the conversation is much less formal than if the same thoughts have been written. Therefore analyzing words that have come through voice recognition have to take into account the informal nature of the words and sentiments that have been expressed.

Fig 2.3 depicts how voice recognition enters textual disambiguation.

Voice transcription

Figure 2.3 From voice transcription to textual disambiguation

There are many factors that affect the quality of the voice transcription. There is the speed a person is speaking. There is the strength of a person's voice. There is the quality and strength of the line that carries the conversation. There is the quality of the recording device. Someone's voice might simply "carries" better than someone else's voice.

But the biggest factor affecting the quality of the transcription is that of the "training" needed before voice transcription can be done. The training involves preparing the system for the accents and colloquialisms that it will hear. There are many accents. There is a New York accent, a Chicago accent, a Georgia accent, and a Texas accent. The voice recognition system needs to be prepared to interpret the kinds of accents that it will be exposed to.

## EMAIL

Another widely used medium for carrying the voice of the customer is that of email. Email is ubiquitous. In some cases the corporation allows/encourages the customer to provide feedback. In other cases email is collected on websites other than the corporation's. In short, the medium of email is found everywhere and is widely used.

In terms of the formality of the language, email is usually more formal than speech and less formal than a written document. Having stated that, emails have a wide variance in the formalism of the expression of thought.

Fig 2.4 shows that email is used to collect information about the voice of the customer.

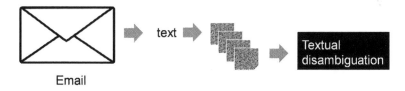

Email

Figure 2.4 Email is used to collect information about the voice of the customer

Email does not suffer from the same quality problems that are found with OCR and voice recognition. About the worst thing that can be said about quality of electronic recognition of emails is that misspellings and slang occur in emails. So email in a sense is much "cleaner" than the other media on which the voice of the customer is found.

However the major challenge with email is managing the sheer volume of data that accompanies email. We can mitigate the huge volume of data found in email by using a "filter" program. The filter program can weed out:

- **Spam.** Spam is unwanted and irrelevant email messages sent into the corporation from outside the corporation.

- **Blather.** Blather is email messages sent inside the corporation which are not relevant to the business of the corporation. As an example of blather, there might be an email from one employee to another that says, "There is a great movie playing Saturday night. Can I pick you up about 6?"

- **System data.** Even highly relevant emails have a lot of system data in them that are not important to or relevant to the intent of the email. The system data is only important to the system and the routing and delivery of the message.

Fig 2.5 shows the challenges related to the processing of email before email arrives at textual disambiguation.

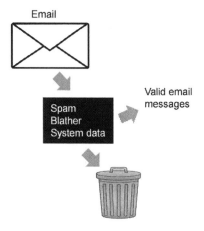

Figure 2.5 Challenges with processing email

## SOCIAL MEDIA

Another place the voice of the customer is heard is in social media. Some typical forms of social media include Facebook, Twitter, Yelp, Open Table, Trip Adviser, Expedia, and Consumer Affairs. There are many different types and formats for social media.

Fig 2.6 shows that social media carries the voice of the customer.

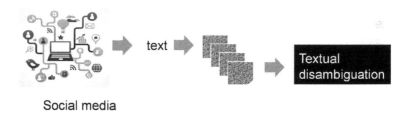

Social media

Figure 2.6 Social media carries the voice of the customer

In many ways, social media is similar to emails in the carrying of the voice of the customer. But there are some subtle differences between social media and standard email processing. Emails can be more direct and to the point and can also carry a lengthy and complex message. Social media on the other hand is indirect and often casual. In addition, social media is often not directed to the corporation about which discussions are being held at all. Many social media messages are directed to the general public.

## SPREADSHEETS

Spreadsheets are great sources for the voice of the customer, although spreadsheets often contain data other than the voice of the customer. On those occasions where the voice of the customer is heard in spreadsheets it usually is fairly formal and direct.

Fig 2.7 shows the voice of the customer that is sometimes found in a spreadsheet.

Figure 2.7 The voice of the customer is sometimes found in a spreadsheet

When the voice of the customer is found in the form of a spreadsheet it is noteworthy that the voice of the customer is found *only* as textual data. Often numeric data is found as the contents of the spreadsheet and when that is the case numeric values almost never express the voice of the customer.

## SURVEYS

Yet another way the voice of the customer is heard is through surveys. While surveys can arrive in a variety of media, there nevertheless are some considerations to be made in hearing the expression of the voice of the customer in a survey. Fig 2.8 shows that surveys can be used to capture the voice of the customer.

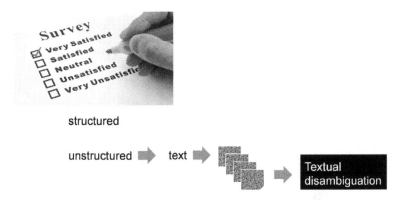

Figure 2.8 Surveys can be used to capture the voice of the customer

Usually surveys have both structured and unstructured modes of allowing the customer to express himself/herself. The structured mode allows the customer to rank feelings by selecting one of several choices. The structured mode is easy to process because it is structured. The problem with the structured portion of a survey is that it presupposes that the person creating the survey knows what the customer wants to say. Sometimes surveys are created well and the customer's thoughts and feelings can be anticipated. But on other occasions the customer's thoughts and sentiments cannot be anticipated. And that is why the unstructured portion of surveys often contains the most valuable information in the survey. It is in the unstructured portion of the survey that the customer has free expression and can truly say whatever is on his/her mind.

Therefore, when trying to hear the voice of the customer, the unstructured portion of a survey becomes the most important part of the survey. It is the unstructured portion of the survey that goes into textual disambiguation.

## WARRANTY CLAIMS

Another really important place the voice of the customer is heard is in the processing of warranty claims. Corporations that issue and back up a warranty hear the voice of the customer in a way no one else does.

With warranty claims the language is direct, formal and descriptive. Fig 2.9 shows that warranty claims are a really good way to hear the voice of the customer.

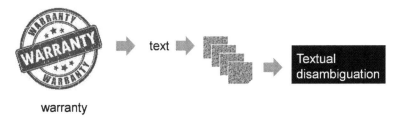

warranty

Figure 2.9 Warranty claims are a good way to hear the voice of the customer

The good news about warranty claims is that the corporation hears first hand and directly about what the customer has to say. The bad news is that the customer only addresses what is wrong with either a service or a product. And the second piece of bad news is that the warranty claim is made after there has been a failure or mishap. Nevertheless the feedback the corporation gets in the processing of warranty claims is truly valuable information.

## PROCESSING THE VOICE OF THE CUSTOMER

As the voice of the customer is being processed, it is worthwhile noting that all of the feedback is freeform. There is little or no predictable text to be found in the processing of the voice of the customer. For this reason, taxonomies and ontologies are widely used to process the voice of the customer. Stated differently, it is very unusual to use inline contextualization in the processing of the voice of the customer.

Fig 2.10 shows that taxonomies and ontologies are used almost exclusively in the processing done by textual disambiguation in the hearing of the voice of the customer. Taxonomies and ontologies work well where there is free form text.

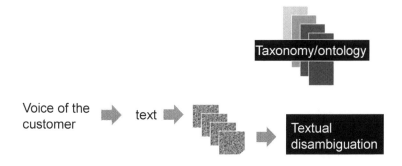

Figure 2.10 Taxonomies and ontologies are used in textual disambiguation

A final note about the processing of the voice of the customer involves a technology called "fuzzy logic". Fuzzy logic says that if the quality of the data is poor, than the quality can be improved by making "educated guesses" as to what the author intended. For example, suppose the following string is found on a document – "Dallas, Te=55". Fuzzy logic might be employed that makes the implication that what was really meant was "Dallas, Texas."

Although fuzzy logic can be employed, experience has shown that fuzzy logic improves the quality of a document by only marginal amounts. In other words you probably won't be disappointed if you use fuzzy logic to improve the quality of a document by 1% or 2%. But you are almost sure to be disappointed if you think that fuzzy logic can improve the quality of the electronic image of a document by 10% or more.

## IN SUMMARY

The voice of the customer arrives in many different forms such as through paper, voice recognition, email, social media, surveys, and warranty claims. Some of the forms the voice of the customer arrives are public, some are private.

When the voice of the customer is heard on paper, technology called OCR must be used. When the voice of the customer arrives by voice, voice transcription technology must be used. In the case of OCR and voice transcription, the quality of the transcription is an issue.

However the voice of the customer is accessed, the voice of the customer is turned into electronic text. Once the voice of the customer is turned into electronic text, it is ready for textual Extract, Transform, and Load (ETL) processing. Developers write code to perform ETL, and often their work is aided by tools that specialize in ETL logic.

# 3: Technology

The organization that hears the voice of their customer on a regular basis and is constantly monitoring what the customer is saying, has an enormous and ongoing advantage over its competitors. That organization has the luxury of being in a proactive stance in the marketplace. So how does an organization go about actually hearing the voice of the customer?

Fig 3.1 shows that there is technology needed to capture, listen to, and analyze what the customer is saying.

Once upon a time, the technology to hear the voice of the customer did not exist or was ineffective. But over time, technology kept improving to the point that today it is absolutely possible to hear the voice of the customer.

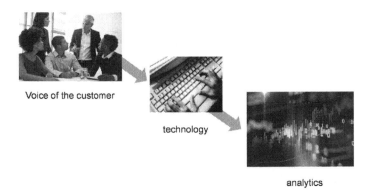

Figure 3.1 Technology is needed to analyze what the customer is saying

The improvements to technology useful for hearing the voice of the customer came on different levels:

- **Cost.** One way improvements in technology have come is in the form of lowered cost of technology. The dramatic drop in cost of technology has afforded the voice of the customer to be heard.

- **Capacity.** The sheer volume of data entailed in hearing the voice of the customer precludes using the technology of yesterday. In order to hear the voice of the customer, it is mandatory that the organization be able to handle very large volumes of data. And with today's technology the organization can do exactly that.

- **Capability.** In an earlier day and age, text was an extremely awkward fit with computing technology. But advances in reading and analyzing text make text as easy to handle today as any other form of data.

## COMPONENTS OF TECHNOLOGY

At a very high level there are four major components to the technology required to hear the voice of the customer, as seen in Fig 3.2.

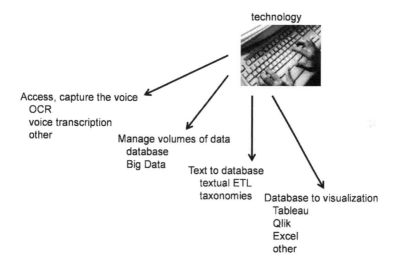

Figure 3.2 Four major components of technology

- **Capture the voice of the customer.** Depending on the form of data that the voice of the customer arrives in, some of the technologies required include OCR and voice transcription. In some cases specialized technology is required for the capture of the voice of the customer. In other cases no special technology is required.

- **Manage volumes of data.** It is simply a truth that in today's world that there is a lot of data out there and that when customers talk, they say quite a bit. Attempting to hear the voice of the customer without being prepared for large volumes of data is a fool's game.

- **Text to database.** In order for the voice of the customer to be analyzed, the text of what is being said must be able to be converted into the form of a standard database. The conversion is really a transformation of text. There is much in the text that must be transformed such as context, sentiment, and the text itself. The technology known as textual ETL along with taxonomies must be deployed.

- **Database to visualization.** Dashboards and other forms of visualization take the data that is in the form of a database and produce a visualization for management's perusal. Once data is served up in the form of a database, the data can be easily and creatively visualized.

## SPECIAL TECHNOLOGY NEEDED

When a customer writes a review on the Internet, there is no special skill or technology needed to capture that instance of the voice of the customer. But on other occasions special technology is required to capture the text. Fig 3.3 shows two instances where special technology is required.

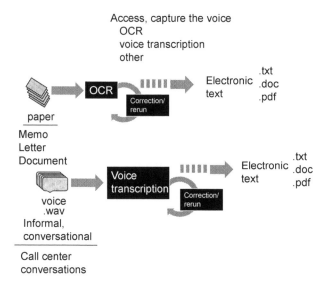

Figure 3.3 Two instances where special technology is required

- **Paper.** Occasionally the voice of the customer arrives in the form of paper. People write letters. People send memos. People take notes. And even though much of the communication done in today's world is done electronically, paper remains a popular medium for communication. When paper is used, OCR allows the paper to be read and the writing on the paper to be transformed into electronic text.

- **Recording.** The other occasion where the voice of the customer must be captured is the case where the customer's voice is recorded. Typical of recordings are call centers and direct customer interchanges. The fact that recordings are used for call centers means that voice to text technology is very important. If there is one arena where the voice of the customer is heard loudly, it is in the corporate call center. Like OCR, the issue with voice to text transformation is in the quality of transformation. If the transformation is not done with a reasonably high degree of accuracy, then the voice of the customer cannot be heard.

There is one other major difference between OCR and voice to text transcription that is worth noting: people talk differently than they write. When writing, people use a more formal approach to develop an idea. But when people talk, the development of ideas is much less formal. People use antecedent references liberally when talking that they would never use when writing. This difference between writing and talking shows up in the interpretation of the text that shows up in the analysis of the voice of the customer.

After capturing text on paper and voice recordings, the next step is the conversion into an electronic format.

## No Special Technology Needed

While some forms of the voice of the customer require technology to convert the text into a form of electronic text, other forms of the voice of the customer do not require any special technology. Typical of the forms of the voice of the customer that do not need any special capture technology are emails, surveys, warranties, and direct customer feedback. Fig 3.4 shows that a lot of the voice of the customer needs no special technology for capture.

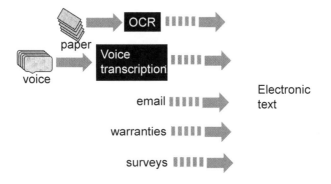

Figure 3.4 A lot of the voice of the customer needs no special technology for capture

## VOLUMES OF DATA

Upon starting to gather the data that constitutes the voice of the customer, one quickly notices that volumes of data start to accumulate. Even for a small business, there is a lot of data that is entailed in the voice of the customer.

Typically there are three places that data starts to accumulate. The first place is standard disk storage. Standard disk storage is a convenient place to look at data that is found on the immediate basis. Looking at this week's voice of the customer or even this month's voice of the customer may be satisfactory when the data is stored on standard disk storage. But when you start to look at the voice of the customer over a lengthy period of time, standard disk storage is soon over run.

Soon data starts to overflow. There are two places where data typically overflows to – Big Data and/or archival storage. By putting the voice of the customer data off to Big Data and/or archival storage the organization can accumulate years of the voice of the customer data.

It is often very useful to store the voice of the customer data over time. In doing so the organization can start to see and quantify changes over time. Fig 3.5 shows the types of storage that can be used to store large amounts of data.

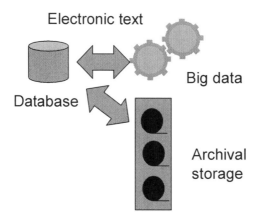

Figure 3.5 Types of storage that can be used to store large amounts of data

A question may arise – why not put all voice of the customer data in a single form of storage? You can try to store large amounts of the voice of the customer data in standard storage. However it is expensive and unwieldy to do so.

Or you can try to store all of your voice of the customer data in Big Data. The problem with storing all of your voice of the customer data in Big Data is that Big Data is not as agile or as flexible as standard data storage.

When looking at the storage requirements for listening to the voice of the customer, there are two obstacles:

- Storage can be expensive, especially when you are talking about the amount of storage that is required to manage the voice of the customer.

- The sheer volume of data that can be generated can make it difficult to read and analyze the data. As long as there is only a modest amount of data, managing the technology is not a particularly large challenge.

## CONVERTING TEXT INTO A DATABASE FORMAT

The next technological challenge in the hearing the voice of the customer is that of converting text into a standard database format. The conversion has long befuddled technicians. There are many facets to the conversion. The most difficult facet to the conversion of text to a database format is the fact that in order for text to be understood, text must be converted along with context.

The problem with context is that in most cases context exists entirely outside the words that are being spoken. In most cases the words themselves give no clue as to the context of their meaning. As text is being converted into a database, the text needs to have its context determined as well.

The process of converting text into a database is a complex process. There are many reasons for the complexity. But among the primary reasons is that there is no one way to determine the context of the text. Some of the techniques used to determine the context of text include:

- Taxonomy resolution
- Homograph resolution
- Inline contextualization
- Custom variable resolution
- Proximity analysis
- Negativity inference
- Sentiment analysis
- Declarative analysis

Fig 3.6 shows the transformation from text into a standard database.

The net effect of the transformation is the transformation of raw text into a standard database management system. The data in the database contains information about text, context, and structure of the voice of the customer.

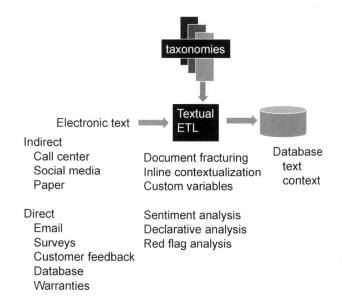

Figure 3.6 The transformation from text into a standard database

Fig 3.7 shows the transformation in a simplistic form.

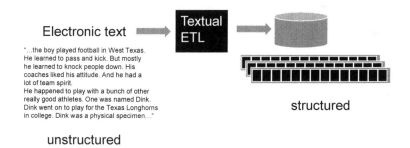

Figure 3.7 The transformation in a simplistic form

One of the primary components necessary to the conversion of text to database is the existence of and usage of a taxonomy. There are many facets to a taxonomy, as shall be discussed in detail in the next chapter.

There are many ways to classify text. One such way is between predictable text and unpredictable text.

## UNPREDICTABLE TEXT

Most text is unpredictable. Unpredictable text is text that is written or spoken in any order. There is no predictability of unpredictable text. A classical example of unpredictable text is an email. You can say anything you want in an email. There are no rules or conventions as to what is said in an email. The contents of an email are unpredictable.

However, there is text that is predictable. In predictable text, there is an order to the text. An example of predictable text is a contract. In many contracts the lawyer merely "boilerplates" the contract. One contract is the same as any other contract with the exception of the name and address of one of the parties to the contract. In predictable text, there indeed is predictability of text.

The taxonomy plays a particularly important role in the conversion of raw unpredictable text into a database. Two of the more important roles that taxonomies play is to allow unpredictable text to be read and understood and to supply much context for the text itself.

## PREDICTABLE TEXT

With predictable text, another very different technique for interpretation and contextualization is required.

As a simple example of predictable text, consider the example for a part of a contract.

Predictable text

"...the undersigned Bill Inmon do solemnly swear to tell..."

In the example there is a predictable beginning delimiter and a predictable ending delimiter. The beginning delimiter is "the undersigned" and the ending delimiter is "do solemnly swear." The text found within the beginning delimiter and the ending delimiter is called the "predicate". In the case, the words "Bill Inmon" are the predicate, as shown in Fig 3.8.

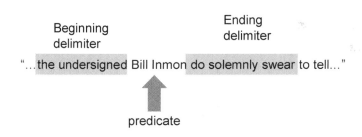

Figure 3.8 The beginning delimiter and the ending delimiter and the predicate

## VISUALIZATION

Once the database is built, the final step is to create a visualization of the database. In the visualization of the database, management can see trends and exceptions. A well-designed visualization makes the important data in the visualization to "pop out".

Typical tools designed for visualizations include Tableau, Qlik, and Excel, among others.

A typical feature of visualizations is the ability to support "drill down" processing.

## IN SUMMARY

In order to turn the text that makes up the voice of the customer into a visualization, a technological transformation is required. There are four major technological technologies that are necessary: the capture of text when the text is not in the form of electronic text, the ability to manage large volumes of text, the ability to turn text into a database, and the ability to visualize a database.

# 4: Taxonomies

When one enters the world of listening to the voice of the customer, new approaches and new technologies are the first thing that is noticed. One of those new technologies is that of taxonomies.

In its simplest form a taxonomy is nothing more than a classification of words. When you look more deeply into a taxonomy, you see that there are different kinds of taxonomies. In particular there are generic taxonomies and specific taxonomies.

## GENERIC VS SPECIFIC TAXONOMIES

A generic taxonomy is a taxonomy that applies anywhere. For example, sentiment is a form of generic taxonomy. It does not matter whether you are talking about cookies and cake, automobiles, sports, or finance.

How you express feelings is all the same for any subject you are speaking about. You can say:

- "...I like ..."
- "... I hate ..."
- "... I despise ..."
- " ...I love ..."

and similar expressions. All phrases express sentiment (either good or bad) and it does not matter what subject you are talking about. The same goes for negativity. The words:

- "...not..."
- " ...no..."
- " ...never..."
- "...hardly..."

all express a negation of what is being said with no regard for the content of what was being expressed. For this reason the words contained in a generic taxonomy are not specific to any one subject.

The other type of taxonomy is a specific taxonomy, which is a taxonomy where the contents are specific to a particular subject. A specific taxonomy is often unique to an industry. Some examples of a specific taxonomy are:

**Golf:**
- Score
- Par
- Birdie

- Eagle
- Bogey
- Course
- Rough
- Green
- Fairway
- Trap

**Or law enforcement:**

- Law breaker
- Felon
- Thief
- Murderer
- Sentence
- Probation
- Hard time
- Release
- Parole

In each of these different venues there are words that have a specific meaning within the context of the venue. Take the word "bird." A golfer thinks of a bird as something quite different from an ornithologist. Each environment – business, commerce, manufacturing, sales, shipping – has its own vocabulary and vernacular. Words that mean one thing in one place mean something entirely different somewhere else. Fig 4.1 shows these two types of taxonomies.

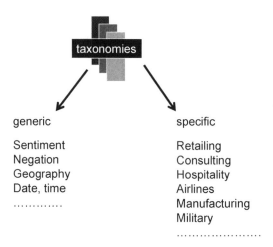

Figure 4.1 Different kinds of taxonomies

As a simple example of a taxonomy, consider the words shown in Fig 4.2. The words shown in Fig 4.2 are part of a larger taxonomy. The taxonomy is for words that might occur inside a call center. In this taxonomy, there are two types of words: categorical words and specific words. The categorical words are on the left of the taxonomy. The categorical words seen in the figure include policy, phone call, red flag, and politeness.

The specific words are seen on the right of the taxonomy. The specific words of politeness include words such as thank you, good morning, good afternoon, and just one minute.

Another category of words are red flag words. Red flag words include such words as emergency, glitch, dispute, trouble, and obstacle.

## A taxonomy for call centers

| | |
|---|---|
| phone_call | question |
| phone_call | phone call |
| policy | gap protection |
| policy | cancellation |
| policy | policy |
| polite | copy all |
| polite | patience |
| polite | thanks |
| polite | i help |
| polite | thank you |
| polite | welcome |
| polite | good afternoon |
| polite | good morning |
| polite | hang on a minute |
| polite | so far so good |
| polite | just one minute |
| polite | [ okay ] |
| polite | [ ok ] |
| red_flag | problem |
| red_flag | glitch |
| red_flag | scare |
| red_flag | sick |
| red_flag | dilemma |
| red_flag | dispute |
| red_flag | headache |
| red_flag | obstacle |
| red_flag | trouble |
| red_flag | disagreement |
| red_flag | catastrophe |
| red_flag | disaster |

Figure 4.2 Simple example of a taxonomy

## TAXONOMY DEPTH

Taxonomies have different "levels". The level of depth of a taxonomy refers to how deep the classifications of data can go. At the very least a taxonomy is two levels deep. In a taxonomy that is two levels deep, there is a simple classification and the words that are classified. In a three level taxonomy there is a classification and a classification of the classification. In an "n" level taxonomy, the classification process can continue as deeply as the analyst wishes. There is no theoretical limit to the depth of an n level taxonomy. There are of course practical limitations. Fig 4.3 depicts a two level, a three level and an n level taxonomy.

| Two level | Three level | N level |
|---|---|---|
| Car | USA | Food |
|   Porsche |   Texas |   Beverage |
|   Volkswagen |     Lubbock |     Soda |
|   Ford |     Dallas |       Coke |
|   Honda |     El Paso |       Diet |
|   Buick |   New Mexico |         classic |
| |     Santa Fe |   Pasta |
| |     Albuquerque |     Italian |
| |     Taos |       Spaghetti |
| |   Utah |         Chef Boyer De |
| |     Salt Lake City |         Canned |
| |     Provo |         Packaged |
| | |     Greek |

Figure 4.3 Different levels of taxonomies

## MULTI LINGUAL TAXONOMIES

Just as there are multiple languages, there are multi lingual taxonomies. A taxonomy can be in English, Spanish, Portuguese, Mandarin, Portuguese, or any other language. Fig 4.4 shows some simple taxonomies in different languages.

| English | | Spanish | |
|---|---|---|---|
| Food | meat | Comida | carne |
| Food | bread | Comida | pan |
| Food | vegetable | Comida | vegetal |
| Food | cake | Comida | pastel |

| French | | Hungarian | |
|---|---|---|---|
| Nourriture | viande | Elelmiscer | hus |
| Nourriture | pain | Elelmiscer | kenger |
| Nourriture | legume | Elelmiscer | zoldseg |
| Nourriture | gateau | Elelmscer | torta |

Figure 4.4 Simple taxonomies in different languages

## OTHER FORMS OF TAXONOMIES

In its simplest form a taxonomy is merely a classification of words. However there are different forms of a taxonomy. One variation of a taxonomy is an acronym table. An acronym table is an acronym and the translation of the acronym. Fig 4.5 shows an acronym table.

A more sophisticated form of an acronym table is a homograph table. In a homograph table there are acronyms. However the same acronym can have multiple translations depending on the context of the word.

Acronyms

Awol   away without official leave
Asap   as soon as possible
Dmz    demilitarized zone
Snafu  situation normal all fouled up

Figure 4.5 An acronym table

As a simple example of a homograph table consider:

HA

- Heart attack when spoken by a cardiologist
- Hepatitis A when spoken by an endocrinologist
- Headache when spoken by a general practitioner

## DYNAMICS OF A TAXONOMY

As interesting as taxonomies are, they are most useful when used to start to dissect and analyze raw text. Taxonomies apply to unpredictable text. When an analyst encounters unpredictable text (and, at the end of the day most text is unpredictable), it is taxonomies that are used to start to understand the text. Fig 4.6 shows a simple example of how taxonomies are applied to raw text.

|  | Car | Dog |
|---|---|---|
|  | porsche | scottie |
|  | ferrari | daschund |
|  | ford | westie |
|  | volkswagen | poodle |
|  | honda | collie |

Raw text
"...she drove her porsche at full speed. Her poodle sat in the back seat, terrified of the speed..."

Textual search
"...she drove her porsche at full speed. Her poodle sat in the back seat, terrified of the speed..."

Post processing
"...she drove her porsche/car at full speed. Her poodle/dog sat in the back seat, terrified of the speed..."

Figure 4.6 A simple example of how taxonomies are applied to raw text

In the first sentence in the example there is raw text about a woman driving her car and her dog. The raw text could be anything. In the second sentence, two taxonomies have been selected: one for cars and one for types of dogs.

The raw text is examined. Each word in the raw text is compared to the specific words in the taxonomy. Two of the raw words are seen to have a match, "Porsche" and "poodle".

In the third sentence the words that are matched have their general classification attached to the specific word.

In this case the words "Porsche" and "poodle" are transformed to "Porsche/car" and "poodle/dog."

The value of classifying raw words is hardly obvious from this simple example. In actuality there are *many* benefits that accrue from taxonomical classification. But there is one immediate benefit that becomes obvious. By doing the processing that has been described, the analyst can look for cars and dogs with a query. And note that in the raw text the words "car" and "dog" are nowhere to be found.

## IN SUMMARY

A taxonomy is a classification of words. Taxonomies are extremely useful in the analysis of raw unpredictable text. When analyzing raw text, the raw text is read and each word in the raw text is used for a search of the applicable taxonomies.

Taxonomies can be divided into two classes: generic and specific. A generic taxonomy is a classification of words that are applicable to any subject and a specific taxonomy is a classification of words that are unique to an industry. Taxonomies can be found in multiple languages and exist at different levels. An n level taxonomy is a taxonomy whose depth of classification goes down an indeterminate number of levels.

# 5: Text

Text comes in all sizes and shapes. There can be long sets of comments and short sets of comments. There can be misspellings, slang, foul language, and colloquialisms.

So how is text read and interpreted? What does textual ETL do in order to turn raw text into a database?

In order to see how text is processed, consider some sample text that was randomly chosen:

> I am so bummed to say this, but this was the worst experience we have ever had at your restaurant. We came here for my husband's birthday with high hopes. We're used to being greeted with the famous cheesy biscuits, but they didn't come to our table till appetizer service (which took 20 minutes).
>
> The server argued with me about a Long Island having sour mix added (he was saying it didn't),

*and then goes on to tell us he's being trained as a bartender.*

*We ordered the shrimp artichoke dip, and it showed up to our table boiled over in the sides and burnt on the rim. There was absolutely 0 flavor, and tasted like thick milk with shrimp in it. We ordered the linguine and the New Orleans shrimp/salmon dish and couldn't even finish it.*

*First off, I received an entire lettuce end in my salad that had no dressing. My salmon was extremely dry, and had almost a burnt pepper crust on top. My husband's linguine was awful. He ALWAYS finishes his food, and couldn't stomach it. We came home feeling sick and extremely disappointed.*

The first observation is that there are different types of sentences found in a comment. There are statements of sentiment and there are declarative statements. A statement of sentiment expresses a like or dislike. A declarative statement is merely a statement of fact where there is no implication of feeling. Fig 5.1 shows the different kinds of statements.

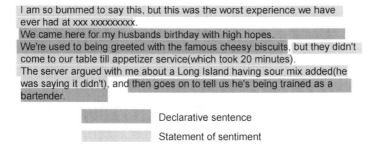

Figure 5.1 Declarative statements and statements of sentiment

The analyst knows how to separate the sentences by passing the sentiment taxonomy against the sentence. If a word or phrase expressing positive or negative sentiment is found in the sentence, then the sentence is deemed to be a statement of sentiment. If the sentence does not contain a statement of sentiment then it is a declarative sentence. In doing sentiment analysis, only sentences that are statements of sentiment are considered.

Note that a comment may contain both positive and negative sentiments in the comment. There may be a sentence like "The fish was too salty but the dessert was yummy." This sentence contains two statements of sentiment. A person can like one thing and dislike something else and there is no contradiction.

## CONNECTORS

Most analysis is based on what is in a sentence. But occasionally a connector binds together two sentences. Fig 5.2 shows the use of a connector.

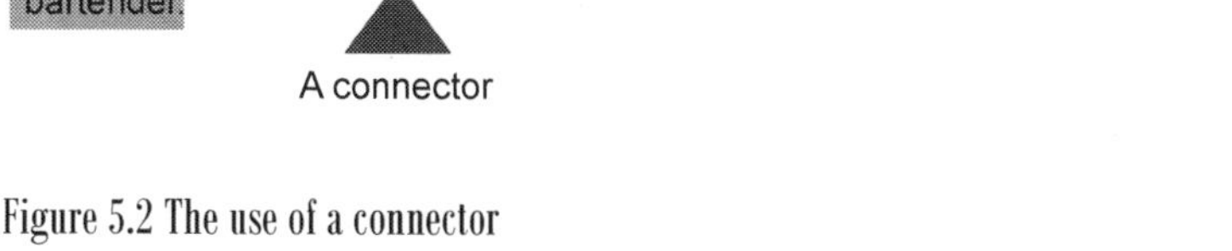

The server argued with me about a Long Island having sour mix added(he was saying it didn't), and then goes on to tell us he's being trained as a bartender

A connector

Figure 5.2 The use of a connector

When a connector is found to separate two or more sentences, the sentences are analyzed separately.

## PREDICATES

A statement of sentiment may contain a predicate. A predicate is merely the object that has a relationship to the sentiment. Sometimes the predicate is the cause of the sentiment. On other occasions, the predicate is the result of the sentiment. Sometimes there may be no predicate at all. Consider the sentence "I am really mad." There is no predicate in this sentence, yet it is definitely a statement of sentiment. Fig 5.3 depicts a statement of sentiment and a predicate.

Negative sentiment
▼
The server argued with me about a Long Island having sour mix added(he was saying it didn't),
▲

predicate

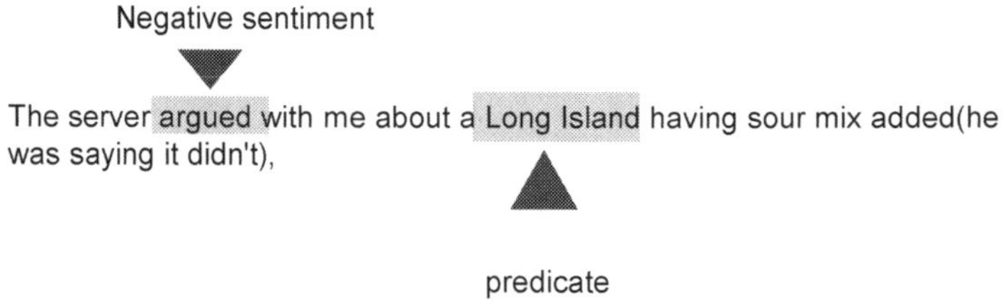

Figure 5.3 A statement of sentiment and a predicate

## COMPLEX SENTENCES

Most sentences are fairly straightforward, but some sentences can be complex. Fig 5.4 shows a sentence that has been made more complex by using parentheses.

The server argued with me about a Long Island having sour mix added(he was saying it didn't),

Complex structure

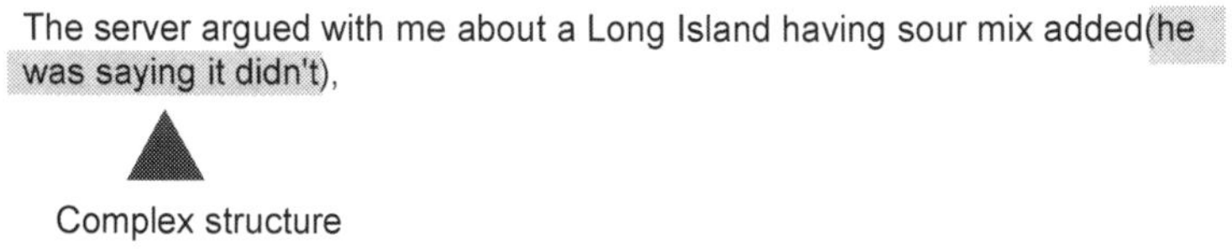

Figure 5.4 A sentence that has been made more complex by using parentheses

# NEGATIVES

In addition to the complexity that can occur naturally in language, the usage of negatives must be accounted for. Fig 5.5 shows the occurrence of a negation.

The server argued with me about a Long Island having sour mix added(he was saying it didn't),

Negation

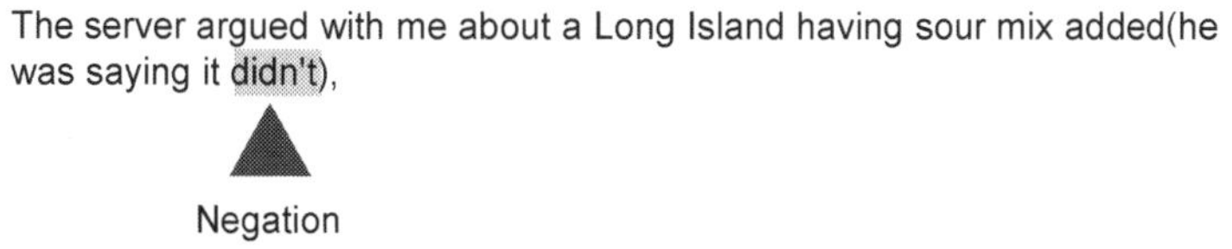

Figure 5.5 The occurrence of a negation

In general negations reverse the meaning of sentiment. Typical words of negation include no, not, never, none, and hardly.

In addition, certain words of sentiment are inherently negative, such as hate, dislike, disgust, and abhor.

So what is the implication when a negation is encountered with a positive sentiment word?

Here is an example:

"I don't like ice cream..."

The word "don't" is recognized as a negation and the word "like" is recognized as a statement of positive sentiment. When analyzing the sentence, the result is a negative statement.

However, when a negation is used in conjunction with an inherently negative word, the implication is that a positive statement has been made. Consider this sentence:

*"I don't dislike raw oysters...."*

The word "don't" is recognized as a negation. And the word "dislike" is recognized as an inherently negative statement of sentiment. The net result of the sentence is interpreted as a positive statement.

## SCOPE OF INFERENCE

The scope of inference refers to all the predicates to which a statement of sentiment applies. Consider the sentence seen in Fig 5.6.

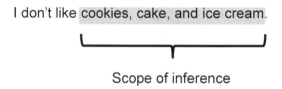

Scope of inference

Figure 5.6 Scope of inference

In the sentence shown in Fig 5.6, the inference of the statement of sentiment is that there are three predicates: cookies, cake, and ice cream. The interjection of a connector is merely a way of showing the continuance of the string of predicates.

The role of the connector is quite different in the sentence shown in Fig 5.7.

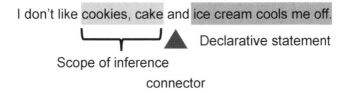

I don't like cookies, cake and ice cream cools me off.

Scope of inference connector

▲ Declarative statement

Figure 5.7 Different role of connector

Even though the sentences in Fig 5.6 and Fig 5.7 are very similar, the role of the connector is very different. In Fig 5.6, the connector is used as a continuance of the predicate. In Fig 5.7, the connector connects a declarative statement to a statement of sentiment.

It is the job of textual ETL to read the sentences, make sense of them, and then to translate the sentences into the form of a database.

## SUPERCATEGORIES

When analyzing sentences and sentiment, it is usually advantageous to organize the comments into different categories called "supercategories." The typical supercategories usually include:

- Person
- Place
- Product
- Price
- Promotion
- Process

- Company
- Ambience

The usual way to determine which supercategory a statement belongs in is by examining and classifying the predicate. The reason why we classify into supercategories is to aid analysis.

## WHAT IS A PRODUCT?

The term product will be different for every company. For example, product in the context of a hotel refers to the hotel itself, to the hotel room, the pool the hotel has, the beach the hotel is on (if the hotel is on a beach), and the lobby of the hotel. In the case of a theater, the product is the seat the viewer sits in, the movie that is playing, and the food counter where candy and popcorn is sold. In the case of an automobile manufacturer, the product is the car that is manufactured and any parts that are manufactured independently. So the product can take on different meanings, as shown in Fig 5.8.

| product | | | |
|---|---|---|---|
| (hotel) | (theater) | (car manufacturer) | (pharmaceutical) |
| Hotel | Movie | Automobile | Pill |
| Hotel room | Seat | Parts | Package |
| Pool | Lobby | .............. | Instructions |
| Elevator | Food counter | | .................. |
| Lobby | .................. | | |
| ........ | | | |

Figure 5.8 A product can take on different meanings

## DRILL DOWN ANALYSIS

Once the raw data has been passed through the taxonomy, it is organized in a hierarchical structure. This hierarchical structure facilitates a drill down analysis. Fig 5.9 depicts an example of drill down analysis.

Figure 5.9 An example of drill down analysis

The first step in the drill down process is to look at sentiment based on the supercategory of data. The analyst finds that hotel room is one of the major components of product for the hotel. The analyst then asks to see what about the hotel room that people are complaining about. The drill down process then takes the analyst to the shower in the hotel room. Continuing the drill down process the analyst finds that the shower is running only cold water.

By doing the drill down process, the analyst has isolated precisely what product is causing the problem, therefore providing much value to the organization.

In the first step of drill down processing the analyst gets to see a high level perspective of the sentiment shown by the customers. The top level view of sentiment is really a broad brush perspective of what customers think. It is a collective view. By looking at the collective view of what customers are saying, management is in a position to "see the big picture."

Then by drilling down, management sees a finer and a finer view of the feedback from the customer. In this case, management can invest some money in the plumbing of the hotel to insure guests get adequate hot water.

## IS THERE TEXT THAT CANNOT BE ANALYZED?

The preceding discussion has discussed general considerations about how text can be analyzed and turned into a database. Indeed most text can be analyzed using the techniques described.

But is it possible that there is text that defies conventional analysis? The answer is absolutely yes.

Consider the writing of two world famous writers, William Faulkner and Ernest Hemingway. Both writers are famous and successful.

However from a writing style the two writers could not be more disparate. Faulkner had a style where his sentences were gargantuan. For example, there is a long paragraph that Faulkner wrote that was one sentence and can be very difficult to understand. Hemingway on the other hand wrote in a clear, simple style. There is very little doubt about what Hemingway was saying.

Trying to use textual ETL on Faulkner-style writing probably would produce very little value. It is inevitable that faced with a sentence from Faulkner there would be mistakes in interpretation. However textual ETL could most likely analyze sentences from Hemingway.

## IN SUMMARY

Customer feedback comes in the form of comments. Comments have two kinds of sentences: statements of sentiment and declarative statements.

Occasionally a connector is used to join two or more sentences together. It is possible for there to be statements of sentiment with different values, one positive and one negative. Some statements of sentiment are inherently negative. Both negations and the inherent attitude of the statement must be considered in order to determine the meaning of the sentence.

It is useful to organize the statements of sentiment according to supercategories. Typical supercategories include person, place, product, process, price, promotion, and company.

Most but not all sentences can be interpreted properly by textual ETL.

# 6: Visualization

Consider the world of the manager. There are a thousand pieces of information and a thousand people vying for the attention of the manager. Management does not have the time to sift through massive amounts of complexity and detail. Visualization allows the manager to cover wide amounts of informational territory in a single glance. As such, visualization allows management to optimize their precious time.

Through visualization, management greatly reduces the amount of time needed to understand the vital numbers that are used to run the organization. While surveying wide amounts of information is the first job of management, occasionally it is necessary to drill down and find the needle in the haystack. Often, visualizations focus on summary data typically over a long period of time. By looking at summary data over a long period of time, management may be able to quickly and easily spot where the needles in the haystack are hiding. Fig 6.1 shows that visualization greatly assists management to find the needles in the haystack.

Figure 6.1 The needle in the haystack

Visualizations help find important business patterns. Many times patterns are not obvious until they are properly visualized. Fig 6.2 shows that visualizations make patterns obvious.

Figure 6.2 Finding patterns

Another way that visualizations are useful to management is in terms of finding exceptions. Fig 6.3 shows that visualizations often times bring out the exceptions.

Figure 6.3 Finding exceptions

Visualizations greatly assist management in surveying large vistas of information in a short amount of time.

## VISUALIZING THE VOICE OF THE CUSTOMER

The requirements for the visualization are the same for the voice of the customer as they are for any other data to be presented to management. So exactly how does the analyst transform the voice of the customer into a visualization? Fig 6.4 shows the path from the capture of the voice of the customer to visualization.

The first step is the capture of the voice of the customer. The next step is the transformation of the voice of the customer into a standard database. The next step is the storage of the data into a standard database. And the fourth step is the reading and analysis of the database and the transformation of the data into a visualization.

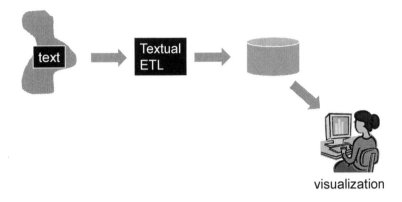

visualization

Figure 6.4 The path from the capture of the voice of the customer to visualization

There are many different kinds of technologies that are capable of reading a database and turning that database into a visualization. Some of the popular visualization pieces of software include Tableau, Qlik, and Excel.

## EXPECTATION PHENOMENON

In most cases reading and interpreting a visualization is a straightforward exercise. But in some cases that is not true. Very quickly the analyst encounters what can be called the "expectation phenomenon."

In order to explain the expectation phenomenon, consider Fig 6.5 which shows a visualization of customer sentiment. The legend says that negative comments are in red and positive comments are in green.

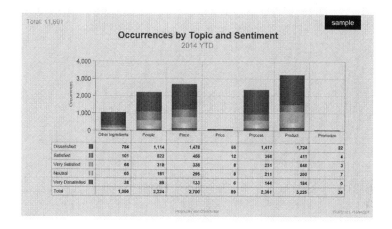

Figure 6.5 A visualization of customer sentiment

It appears that there are many more negative comments than positive. But there is a rational explanation for this. Suppose you go into a restaurant with your family to have a meal. You have a wonderful meal and you leave the restaurant happy and satisfied. When that is your experience, do you provide any feedback? Usually not. You went into the restaurant expecting to have a good experience and the restaurant met your expectations.

Now suppose you go into a restaurant and you have a bad experience. The food was bad. Or the waitress was snippy. Or the table wasn't clean. Something about the restaurant and the meal did not meet your expectations. You therefore post a negative review. Because the vast majority of people who go into a restaurant have their expectations met, the ratio of positive to negative comments is skewed. It is only when our expectations are not met that we voice a complaint. Fig 6.6 shows the analysis of positive comments to negative comments for a really well run organization.

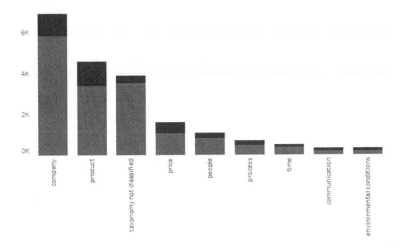

Figure 6.6 The sign of a really well run organization

Indeed, there are negative comments seen in Fig 6.7. However the ratio of positive to negative comments shows that nearly all of the customers are happy. It is of note that different industries have different ratios of positive to negative comments. As a rule for a restaurant a ratio of 15% to 85% of positive to negative is the norm.

## THE IMPORTANCE OF NEGATIVE FEEDBACK

Negative feedback is important. By drilling down on the negative feedback, the organization finds out what the problems with the customer experience are. By drilling down on the negative comments, management is given a blueprint as to exactly what needs to be done to improve the customer experience.

Visualizations are effective because we can see how summarizations and Key Performance Indicators (KPIs) change over time. Trends become easy to spot.

## NON SENTIMENT DATA

Recall there are statements of sentiment and declarative statements. Customer sentiment gets to the heart of the customer voice. Declarative statements may not tell what the customer is feeling, but declarative statements tell what is on the mind of the customer. The customer would not mention a subject in a declarative statement if it were not important to the customer.

To address declarative statements, there is another type of report that is useful in portraying the voice of the customer. That analysis can be called the customer mindset analysis, as seen in Fig 6.7.

Figure 6.7 Customer mindset analysis

## IN SUMMARY

In order to communicate effectively with management, it is necessary to put information in the form of a visualization, as shown in Fig 6.8.

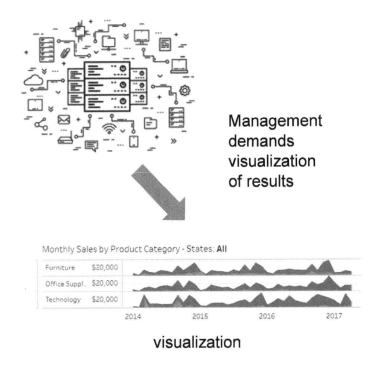

Figure 6.8 Management requires data in the form of a visualization

Interpreting a visualization requires an awareness of the phenomenon of customers making comments based on their expectations being met. While customer sentiment is most important, a close second is understanding the mindset of the customer.

# 7: Restaurants

The restaurant business is competitive. Restaurants are always competing for new customers and trying to hold on to existing ones. Typically restaurants are measured by several parameters:

- Menu
- Ambience
- Service
- Pricing

## THE VOICE OF THE CUSTOMER

Success in managing a restaurant always boils down to one thing: the opinion of the customer. The restaurant can rate itself all it wants in whatever categories it wants. But the only rating and opinion that really counts is that of the customer.

For long term success and health the restaurant needs to listen continuously to what the customer is saying about the restaurant. It is not enough for the restaurant to hear the voice of the customer today. The restaurant must hear the voice of the customer tomorrow, next week, and next month.

Although there are many ways feedback to the restaurant can be accomplished, the most common is over the Internet.

## FEEDBACK OVER THE INTERNET

The Internet is a good medium for hearing what the customer has to say because the customer can be anonymous, as explicit as desired, and can write as long or short a message as desired. As a simple example of the feedback given to a restaurant, consider the following (real) example:

> Product(s): Caesar Salad Parmesan Chicken Breast I have ordered a Caesar Salad with a Parmesan Chicken Breast twice now. Both times, the restaurant neglected to include the chicken in my to go order. Also, today I was given dressing that had separate d. I called and was told that that's just how it was going to be. I love your restaurant and was very disappointed. Not a good experience at all.

Over the course of a month, a restaurant may receive many message similar to this one.

There are many lessons to be learned from looking at customer feedback. But there are two challenges from collecting feedback over the Internet:

- **Volume.** There are so many messages from the customer. In a month's time, there may be 50,000 to 100,000 messages for a good sized restaurant chain. Trying to read and digest 50,000 messages manually is an impossible task.

- **Format.** The messages are in text. The computer does not handle text well. The computer is designed to handle repetitive, transaction activities, where there is a high degree of structure to the activities. And there just is no high degree of repetitivity to be found in text.

## TEXTUAL ETL

Textual ETL can greatly alleviate the challenges facing the organization trying to hear the voice of the customer. The restaurant can actually listen to all of their customers in an accurate and easy to understand manner.

The architectural rendition of how textual ETL works is shown in Fig 7.1.

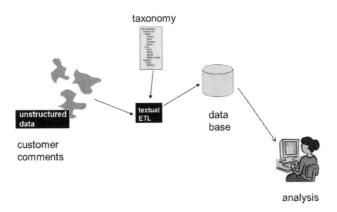

Figure 7.1 The architectural rendition of how textual ETL works

Textual data in the form of customer comments are fed into textual ETL. You can feed as many as you like into textual ETL. Textual ETL then reads, analyzes, and converts the comments into a database. Once the comments have been converted into a database, they can then be analyzed by a standard analytical program. Then management can see what the customer is saying.

## SO WHAT IS THE CUSTOMER SAYING?

As an example of the analysis that can be done, consider the following graph in Fig 7.2.

The graph shown has seven categories: other ingredients, people, place, price, process, product, and promotions. The graph was created from an analysis by textual ETL of thousands of customer comments.

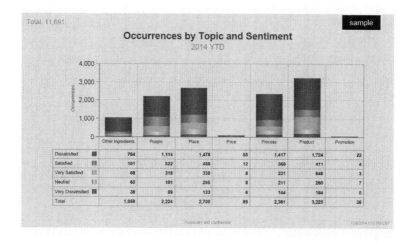

Figure 7.2 An example of the analysis that can be done

In the graph, red indicates a negative comment and green indicates a positive experience. At first glance it appears that there is a lot more negatives comments, which is true. But as we've seen earlier, people often only give feedback when they are dissatisfied so the fact that there are more red than green is not a great concern.

## LEAVING MONEY ON THE TABLE

There is one really remarkable fact that sticks out from this chart. That fact is no one says anything about price. This is an indication that the restaurant chain may be "leaving money on the table." The restaurant chain needs to consider marginally raising prices.

Another interesting fact that comes from this graph is that hardly anyone has anything to say about promotions. In fact, the restaurant chain is doing promotions. But the promotions are having little or no impact. The restaurant should consider doing some other kinds of promotions.

Giving management the message that they should be charging more and that they should be doing more effective promotions, is important news that management should hear.

But there are lots of other pieces of information that can be gleaned from what the customer is saying. Consider the graph in Fig 7.3.

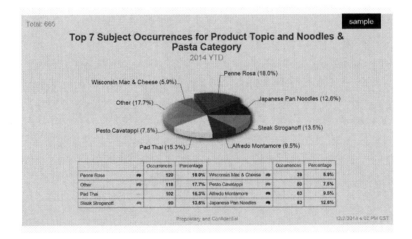

Figure 7.3 The different dishes in the pasta category mentioned by the customer

The most mentioned dish was penne rosa and the least mentioned dish was Wisconsin macaroni and cheese. This graph shows what was on the mind of the customer after having a dining experience.

## DRILL DOWN PROCESSING

There is other important information that can be gleaned. You can drill down on any given dish. For example, you could take a closer look at Pad Thai, as shown in Fig 7.4.

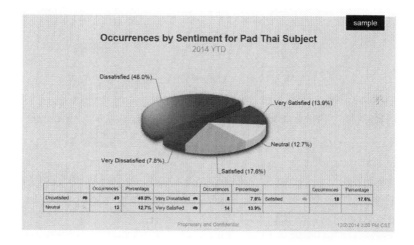

Figure 7.4 Taking a closer look at Pad Thai

When you drill down on Pad Thai you see that most of the comments were expressing dissatisfaction. Continuing your curiosity you ask "Why are people dissatisfied with Pad Thai? Is Pad Thai too spicy? Not spicy enough? Too many noodles? Not enough sauce? What is it about Pad Thai that the customers are not liking?" Figure 7.5 shows that the portion size is the main reason for the customers negative comments to Pad Thai. The restaurant needs to increase the portion size of Pad Thai in order to please the customer.

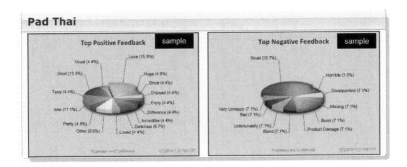

Figure 7.5 Drilling into more detail

Not only is sentiment derived from the customers comments, but the reasons for the sentiment is also derived. This is really powerful information for the manager that wants to increase customer satisfaction.

Another way to look at information is by information over time. Once the data has been put into a database, it can be analyzed over time. See Fig 7.6.

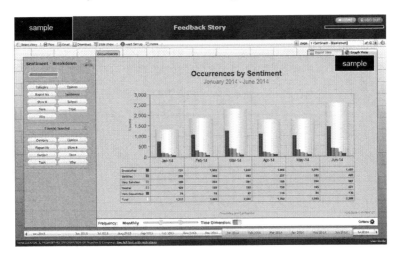

Figure 7.6 Information over time

Another possibility is looking at customer feedback based on the stores (the physical locations where the the restaurant chain has businesses). See Fig 7.7.

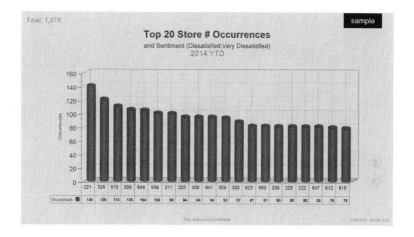

Figure 7.7 Looking at customer feedback based on the stores

In this figure, it is seen that the different locations are ranked by comments per location. It is seen that store 221 has had more feedback than any other store. This may or may not be an indicator of a problem at store 221. It could be that store 221 is in midtown Manhattan and does more business than any other store. Or it could be that there is a real problem with store 221. If this information were married with other corporate information, you could find out whether this is a problem location or whether this location is just large.

In any case, management knowing which locations are well run and which locations need management attention is very valuable information.

Suppose now management wants to find out what exactly is going on in location 221. With the data in a database, they can do exactly that. See Figure 7.8.

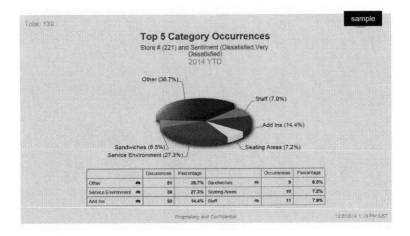

Figure 7.8 What is going on in location 221?

The graph shows that with the data in the form of a database, management can look deeply into what is going on in location 221.

## IN SUMMARY

When you are running a restaurant, hearing what your customers are saying is the key to return business and a solid foundation of loyalty. With the Internet it is now possible to have a direct connection between you and your customers.

And with textual ETL you can put the feedback from the customers in a form that can be analyzed. With the Internet and textual ETL you can:

- Listen to thousands of customers
- Understand text and narrative

Once your data is in the form of a database, you can analyze it many different ways. You can find out sentiment and drill down on any issue you wish. You can find out what locations have the most complaints. You can find out what is behind the complaints.

# 8: Call Centers

Nearly every corporation has a call center. Ask an executive if his/her organization has a call center, and the odds are that the executive will say yes.

Then you ask the executive whether or not he/she knows what is going on in the call center. The executive assures you that they know what is going on in the call center, and tells you the corporation is getting 6,000 calls a day and the average length of the call is 4 ½ minutes.

Now knowing the number of calls and knowing how long the calls have lasted is one interesting measurement of the activity going through the call center. But this kind of information does not tell you anything about the content of what is going on in the call center.

## WHAT YOU WOULD LIKE TO KNOW

Here are some questions that would be useful to answer:

- What are customers complaining about?

- What are customers asking questions about?

- Do customers want to buy something?

- Do customers need more information about operating equipment?

- Are customers having installation problems?

- Are customers interested in further options associated with equipment?

## TEXTUAL ETL

You can answer questions like these using Textual ETL. In order to see just how Textual ETL creates the opportunity for the corporation to start to use the information found in the call center for better decision making, consider the following example.

Fig 8.1 contains the synopsis of call center activity that a telephone company has with its customers. In a day's time, the telephone company will get thousands of phone calls in their call center. The calls are about the many aspects of the day-to-day operation of the telephone company. The telephone company also services television programming.

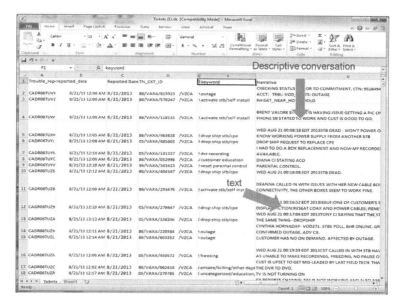

Figure 8.1 The synopsis of call center activity

There is no way that an individual can read all of the messages and assimilate what is being said by the customer. There simply are too many messages. So Textual ETL is used in order to read the textual information of what has transpired in the call center and to assimilate that information.

The conversation information is read by Textual ETL and converted into a database. Once the text has been converted into a database, the database can be read and analyzed.

Depending on the text, different sorts of algorithmic processing inside textual ETL occurs:

- **Stop word processing.** In stop word processing, extraneous words such as "a," "and," "the," "to," and "from" are removed before the data is loaded into the database.

- **Stemming.** Stemming occurs by reducing words to their Greek or Latin stem. The relationship between "move," "moving," "mover," "moves," and "moved" is recognized.

- **Alternate spelling.** A simple example of alternate spelling is recognizing the British spelling of "colour" means the same as the American spelling "color."

- **Taxonomic/algorithmic resolution.** Taxonomic resolution allows words to be classified. A simple example of taxonomic resolution is the recognition that "Honda," "Volkswagen," "Porsche," "Chevrolet," and "Toyota" are all "cars."

- **Homographic resolution.** Homographic resolution occurs when it is recognized that the same word or phrase has different meanings to different audiences. For example, "ha" means heart attack to the cardiologist, hepatitis A to the endocrinologist, and headache to the general practitioner.

- **Proximity analysis.** Proximity analysis is the recognition that words in proximity to each other have different meanings than when the words are separated. For example, "Dallas Cowboys" refers to a football team, whereas "Dallas" on page 1 and "cowboys" on page 4 convey an entirely different meaning.

- **Negation resolution.** Negation resolution refers to the practice of inferring negation of meaning upon encountering a negative term, such as "no," "not," and "never."

- **Date standardization.** One document has "June 5, 2016" and another document has "06/05/2016." In order to be placed into a database, the dates need to be standardized.

## VISUALIZATION

Once the text is read and converted into a database, the database can be read and fed into a visualization tool. The visualization tool can be used to create a dashboard. Fig 8.2 shows a dashboard that can be created.

The dashboard that has been created shows the activities that are occurring inside the call center.

On the top left hand side is the display of the type of calls that are occurring in the call center ranked by the number of calls. Typical of calls are complaints, questions, inquiries about sales, and installation questions. This information tells management the general demeanor of the activities going through the call center.

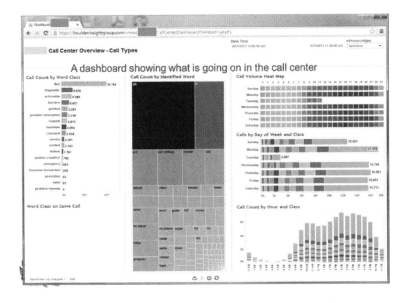

Figure 8.2 Dashboard (Note: This dashboard was created by Boulder Insight.)

On the bottom right hand side is the analysis of phone calls by hour of the day. This diagram shows that there is little or no activity during the hours of 2:00 am and 3:00 am. However during prime time, 9:00 am to 4:00 pm, there is a lot of activity. Furthermore the analyst can drill down on the hour to go to a lower level of detail should deeper analysis be required.

Above the hourly analysis is the daily analysis. The daily analysis shows that different kinds of call center activity have occurred on different days of the week. Above the daily analysis is the monthly analysis.

And finally in the center of the dashboard are the subjects that were contained in the call center analysis. The different subjects that were mentioned by the conversations that occurred in the call center are listed in a demographic manner. The largest and darkest box show the most mentioned subjects. The smaller and lighter boxes show the lesser-mentioned subjects.

The dashboard seen in the figure shows that an organization can know what is occurring in the call center. When someone says, "You can't know what is going on in the call center," that person hasn't seen one of these dashboards.

## PROCESSING TEXT

It is interesting to look at the text to database processing from the standpoint of what the computer sees and what the computer has to do in order to create the database that is behind the dashboard.

First off, what does a textual document look like to the computer? A textual document looks like a long string of text to the computer. It is one word or character followed by another word or character followed by yet another word or character.

A picture of what the computer sees is seen in Fig 8.3.

So what do you need to do to text to turn it into a form that can be analyzed?

Figure 8.3 A picture of what the computer sees

It is up to the computer to read and interpret the long string of text and to take that text as input into the creation of a database. There are currently 67 algorithms that are required to read and interpret text found inside of Textual ETL. Making matters even more complex is the fact that the algorithms have to be sequenced properly for their execution. For example, in some cases for algorithm A to run successfully, algorithm B has to have been executed. And on other occasions, algorithm A has got to be executed before algorithm B is run, all depending on the text that is being processed.

Some of the more common algorithms include:

- Proximity analysis
- Date standardization
- Custom variable formatting
- Inline contextualization
- Taxonomy/ontology resolution

Fig 8.4 shows the application of the algorithm to the text that is input into textual ETL.

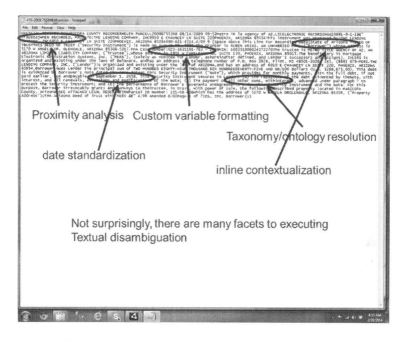

Figure 8.4 The application of the algorithm

## THE RELATIONAL DATABASE

The result of the processing of the text by textual ETL is a relational database. While the creation of a simple relational database is hardly new, to the organization struggling with text the ability to create a relational database represents a significant milestone.

Once the text is turned into a database, there is no limit to the number of documents that can be read and analyzed. Analysis can be done by standard analytical software. Fig 8.5 shows the relational database that has been created from the processing of text by Textual ETL.

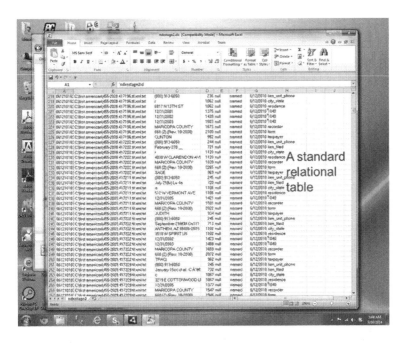

Figure 8.5 The relational database that has been created from the processing of text

Some of the features of the relational database include:

- Identification of the document (or the call center record)

- Byte address of the word being analyzed

- The actual word being analyzed

- The context of the word being analyzed

Fig 8.6 shows some of the features of the database.

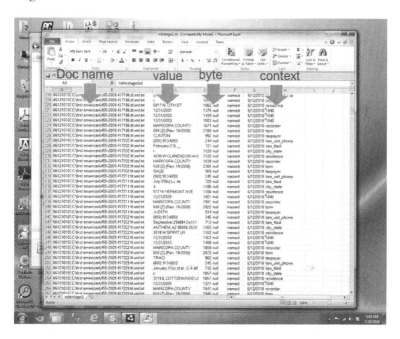

Figure 8.6 Some of the features of the database

While there are many aspects of the data found in the database that are important, one of the unique and most important features of the database is the identification of the context found in the call center. Stated differently, while text is important, context is even more important. Text without context is meaningless.

And context of text is a standard feature of the database produced by Textual ETL. Textual ETL handles both text and context. Fig 8.7 shows that both text and context are found in the database created by Textual ETL.

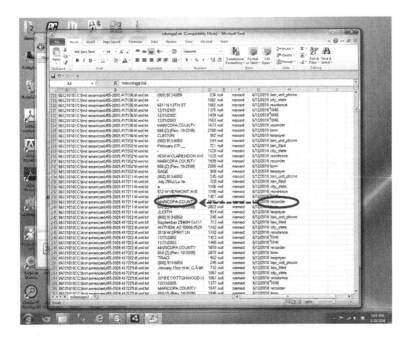

Figure 8.7 Both text and context are found in the database created by Textual ETL

In the figure it is seen that the call center has mentioned the words "Maricopa County". The context of those words is a place where a real estate deed has been recorded.

Note that Maricopa County could have referred to many things. Maricopa County could be:

- A place where professional baseball teams practice in the early season

- A place where a deed was recorded

- A place where a murder occurred

- A place where you took a vacation

- A place where a movie was shot

From an analytical standpoint, it is crucial to capture context as well as text.

## IN SUMMARY

The applicability of Textual ETL is widespread. That is because text is widespread. Textual ETL becomes the key to unlocking the information found in the text within call centers.

# 9: Airlines

It's no secret: the airlines business is competitive. There are fare wars. There are frequent flyer clubs. There are special seat pricing algorithms. There is constant competition among airlines for the customers and the customers' dollars.

At the end of the day, the deciding factor on airline traffic is the customer and who the customer chooses for his or her journey. So how does an airline start to build customer loyalty?

Sure, there are frequent flyer programs. But frequent flyer programs only tell part of the story because every airline has frequent flyer programs. If an airline is really interested in building customer loyalty, the airline can do something: listen to what their customers are saying.

## LISTENING TO THE CUSTOMER

Listening to the customers is simple in concept. The customer speaks and the airline listens. But at the same time, listening to the customer is difficult because:

- There are so many customers

- There are so many ways the customers can speak

- Computers are designed for handling transactions, not language

To try to listen to the customer manually is not a possibility. There simply are too many customers.

Realistically the only way the airline can listen to the passenger is in an automated manner using the computer. One of the best ways for the airline to hear what the customer is saying is to turn to the Internet. When you look at the Internet, there are whole collections of feedback from the passenger. Most of the comments made by the passenger are in the form of complaints.

## GATHERING THE CUSTOMER FEEDBACK

In spring of 2016, a large number of comments were gathered up from a wide variety of websites off the Internet. The information that was gathered was open to the public. The feedback from airline customers was gathered into a textual data set.

The passenger feedback was for the spring of 2016 and the entirety of the year for 2015. The feedback was gathered for both domestic US and for worldwide flights.

The feedback was gathered for all airlines. If an airline only appeared a few times that was because there were only a few mentions of the airline. If the airline appeared many times, that was because the number of complaints against the airline was numerous. There was no effort to either include or exclude the complaints for any airline.

The topics covered by the passengers complaints included anything the passenger had on his/her mind. A typical comment found on the Internet looks like:

On 31.01.2016 I landed at Delhi airport on flight number AI 116 at 2:50am. Unfortunately my baggage did not arrive.

I inquired at the airport and was told that my baggage will arrive at my hotel at 3pm the same day as my luggage was on another flight.

I waited at my hotel until 3pm and my luggage had not arrived. I contacted Air India at Delhi airport and I was told it would arrive at my hotel at 6pm. At 6pm the luggage had still not arrived at my hotel so I contacted Air India at Delhi airport and I was told that it would arrive at my hotel at 9pm. At 9pm the luggage had still not arrived at my hotel so I contacted Air India at Delhi airport and I was told it would arrive at my hotel 9am the next morning. At 9am the next morning my luggage had still not arrived at my hotel.

As shown in Fig 9.1, all of the customer complaints and comments were processed through textual ETL. Other input to textual ETL includes taxonomies appropriate to airlines passengers. A standard database is created. A visualization is then created for the airline passengers complaints.

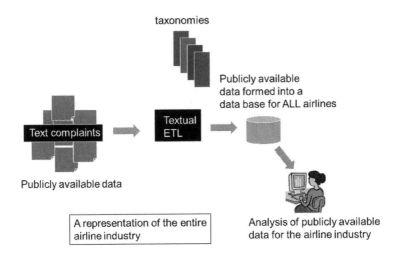

Figure 9.1 The customer complaints and comments were processed via textual ETL

Of special interest is the fact that not only is the sentiment of the passenger captured, but the reason for the sentiment is captured too. The study (visualization by Boulder Insight) looks like the graphic in Fig 9.2.

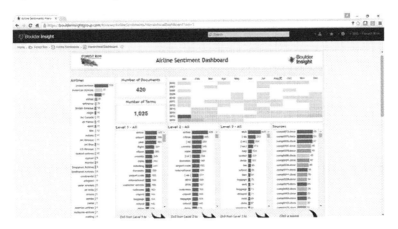

Figure 9.2 Visualization by Boulder Insight

The first column shows the airlines that were mentioned and the order of frequency in which they were mentioned. See Fig 9.3.

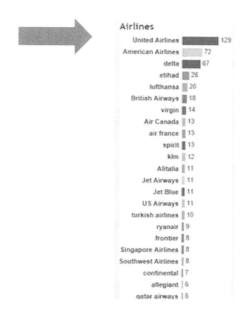

Figure 9.3 The airlines that were mentioned and the order of frequency

The second column shows the subjects that were mentioned by the passengers ranked by the number of times they were mentioned. See Fig 9.4.

The third column shows the sub rankings for any given column.

As with all dashboards there are many ways to look at the data. One such way is to focus on one airline, then to focus on one aspect of the airline. See Fig 9.5.

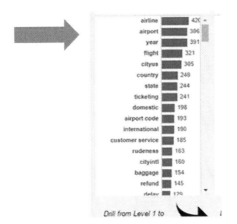

Figure 9.4 The subjects that were mentioned by the passengers

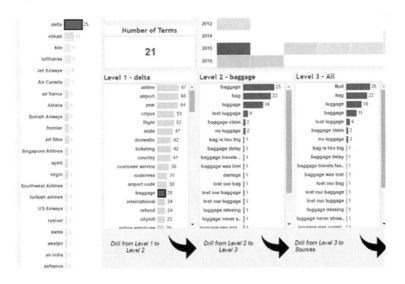

Figure 9.5 Focus on one airline, then focus on one aspect of the airline

In this case the airline chosen is Delta Airlines and the subject that is focused on is luggage. The second column shows the comments made about luggage handling at Delta Airlines.

## IN SUMMARY

By using focus and drill down the analyst can get a much clearer picture of what was being said and why.

Furthermore, drill down can continue all the way down to the actual comment that was used to create the analysis in the first place. See Fig 9.6.

Product: flight cancellation

Company: Delta Airlines

Category: Airlines

Hello,

I'm writing to find out the most effective way of filing a complaint about Delta Airlines.

My name is Basak O, and I am a business traveler who uses Delta's services frequently. However, my latest experience with Delta has been exhausting, disappointing, and painful. I was supposed to be on Delta Flight Number 148 on December 19, 2009; however, due to weather conditions, my flight was canceled. My Delta number was DYOK36. I had to miss a very important meeting; I suffered financial loses; and I was very upset at the rudeness of the Delta personnel at JFK. Then they put me on a direct flight to Istanbul on December 20, 2009, "which was canceled not because of the weather but because the flight attendants could not make it to the airport. Upon hearing this disappointing news, I went to collect my baggage from Delta, but they were unable to find it, although they did make me wait for five hours at JFK. They finally told me that my luggage would be waiting for me in Istanbul. I wanted to speak with a Delta representative to cancel my flight and collect my money back, but there was absolutely no one available. Furthermore, no one picked the telephone for 72 hours at Delta!"

Figure 9.6 Drill down can continue all the way down to the actual comment

While textual ETL can certainly be used for looking at and analyzing publicly available data, Textual ETL can be used to analyze any textual data.

# 10: Surveys

Surveys can be submitted many ways including by mail, over the phone, and over the Internet.

Typically a corporation has a question on the survey. There are two distinct parts to the response: a set of structured checked boxes and a place for a written comment. The set of boxes are arranged in a classical form of structured data and the written responses are a typical form of unstructured data, as seen in Fig 10.1.

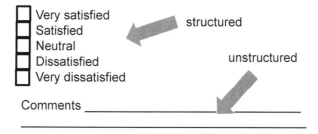

Figure 10.1 Structured and unstructured content on a survey form

The classical form of a response to a survey is very common. But the problem with this very common structure is that the survey assumes it knows what is on the mind of the respondent in constructing the set of boxes. Instead the comments portion of the survey response is where the respondent can tell what really is on the mind of the respondent.

## THE REAL VALUE OF THE SURVEY

The real value of a survey is in terms of the comments made by the respondents. Fig 10.2 shows this very normal occurrence.

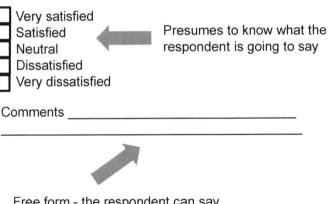

Figure 10.2 The real value of a survey are the comments made by the respondents

So what is the problem with having the value of the survey lie in the response in the comments section of the survey? The problem is that the comments are in the form of text. There are too many comments for one person to read. If a person reads 10,000 comments, the person will do well to remember 5 of them. Stated differently, when there are a lot of comments, they cannot effectively be processed by a human.

However, just because the comments are in the form of text and that there are a lot of them does not mean that the comments cannot be read and analyzed. Fig 10.3 shows how textual ETL can be used to read and process comments from a survey.

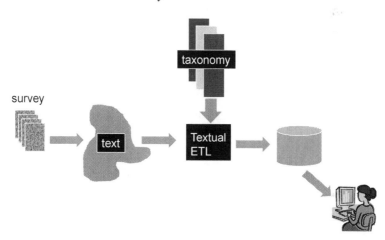

Figure 10.3 How textual ETL can be used to process comments from a survey

In Fig 10.3, it is seen that the text from the survey is lifted and put into the form of electronic text. The electronic text is read and processed by textual ETL. In processing, textual ETL also takes taxonomies as input.

The result of processing is a standard database. Once the survey results are in the form of a standard database, the results can be analyzed and visualized. In such a manner the survey can be another channel for hearing the voice of the customer.

## TAXONOMIES

The taxonomies that are used for processing have a very strong relationship to the surveys. For example, if the survey were for human resources to discover the attitude of the employees of the corporation, the taxonomy would relate to the employees' jobs.

Suppose the survey was for employees of the organization and that organization was a healthcare organization. The taxonomies would relate to hospitals, shift work, doctor and nurses, and patient care. Or suppose the organization was a retailer. The taxonomies would relate to sales people, stockers, cashiers, and buyers. The taxonomies used for a hospital would be very different than the taxonomies used for a retailer.

There is a close relationship between the actual survey and the taxonomies used in the processing of the survey.

## SENTIMENT AND DECLARATIVE STATEMENTS

When one examines the comments in a survey, it is normal to find two kinds of sentences in the comments: statements of sentiment and declarative statements.

When it comes to analyzing the survey comments, two very different kinds of analysis are done: sentiment analysis and mindset analysis.

A simple example of a statement of sentiment is, "I really liked the lamb chops." A simple example of a declarative sentence is, "We went to the restaurant on a Tuesday evening." The statements of sentiment tell about the likes and dislikes of the customer. And the statements of declaration tell about the mindset of the customer. Fig 10.4 shows this type of analysis.

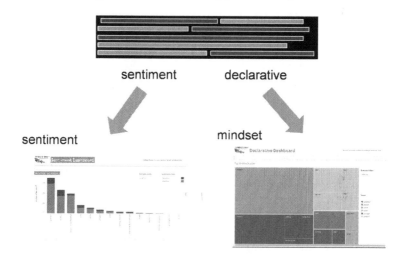

Figure 10.4 Both sentiment and mindset are useful

## DIFFERENT TYPES OF SENTIMENT

One feature of the taxonomy that may or may not be made is the distinction between types of sentiment. For example, the taxonomy may make the distinction between something that is very positive verses something that is merely positive. Or the taxonomy may make the distinction between something that is very negative versus something that is merely negative.

As a simple example consider the following distinctions:

- Very positive – love
- Positive – like
- Negative – dislike
- Very negative – hate

The taxonomy may be divided up into these distinctive categories. In doing so, the voice of the customer can be refined and clarified, as seen in Fig 10.5.

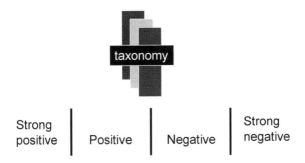

Figure 10.5 The taxonomy may be divided up into distinctive categories

## SEGMENTING THE RESPONDENTS

One of the other useful pieces of information that can occur when doing a survey is that information other than the survey can be gleaned. For example, it may be possible to determine who is doing the survey and where.

Suppose the employees of an airline are being surveyed. It may be useful to divide the survey results up into groups of employees such as pilots, flight attendants, reservations, and gate clerks. Or if the organization were a healthcare organization, it may be useful to divide the groups of people responding into doctors, nurses, administrators, and orderlies.

In addition, if the location of the respondents can be determined, the respondents can be grouped by location. There may be people from the South, people from the West, Northeast, and mid-West. Being able to segment the respondents may lead to some very interesting insights. Fig 10.6 shows that assigning the respondents to different categories can lead to incisive insights.

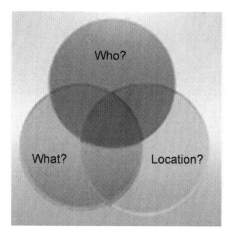

Figure 10.6 Assigning the respondents can lead to incisive insights

## IN SUMMARY

The ubiquitous response form typically has two parts – a structured set of boxes and a place for comments. In many surveys the really interesting information from the survey comes from the comments. The structured set of boxes pre-supposes what the respondent is thinking while the comments form allows for free expression.

There usually are too many responses to a survey for the comments to be read and cogently analyzed by an individual. The way that the comments on a survey can be analyzed is through textual ETL. Textual ETL reads the comments, analyzes them, and places the comments in a standard database. From the database the comments are analyzed and turned into a visualization.

# 11: Strategy

Businesses that seriously listen to the voice of the customer prosper. Their revenues rise. Their stock value rises. They increase the number of their customers. In a word – businesses that listen to their customer flourish.

## STRATEGICALLY AND TACTICALLY

You can listen to your customer strategically or you can listen to your customer tactically (or you can do both). See Fig 11.1.

When you listen to your customer strategically, you listen to your customer all at once, collectively. You listen to thousands of customers and amalgamate their views into a single statement.

When you listen to your customer tactically, you listen to them one at a time, such as in a phone conversation, in an email, and in an office visit.

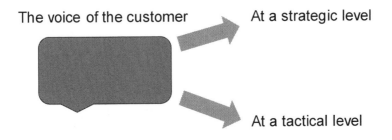

Figure 11.1 The ways you can listen to the voice of your customer

## A CORPORATE BENCHMARK

When you listen to your customer strategically, you can critique your own company as to whether it is well run in the eyes of the customer or whether it is poorly run.

This analysis is done by looking at a sentiment analysis chart and looking at the ratio of positive comments versus negative comments. In a well-run company, the positive comments will outweigh the negative comments. In a poorly run company, the negative comments will outweigh the positive comments. Fig 11.2 shows such a comparison.

The high level overview of the ratio of positive versus negative comments is a good high level measurement of how the company is thought of by its customers.

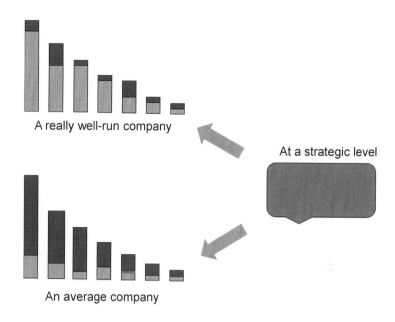

Figure 11.2 Comparing a well-run company with an average company

## WHAT'S ON THE CUSTOMER'S MIND?

A second important use of listening to the customer's voice is in learning what is on the customer's mind. The analyses start with the major categories of information important to the business, such as:

- Person
- Product
- Process
- Price
- Promotion
- Company
- Place

The ranking of these subjects tells management what the customer is especially sensitive to. And the analytical graphs that are produced make it crystal clear as to what topics the customer values. In addition, the manager can see at a glance where the trouble areas are.

The ability to listen to the voice of the customer and to visualize it greatly increases the ability of management to focus on what the customer desires.

Another value in listening to the voice of the customer and visualizing results is the ability to mark progress over time. The organization can visualize the voice of the customer at some point in time, point A. Then the organization can repeat the visualization as of some later point in time, point B. Then the organization can compare the results at point in time A versus point in time B. The visualization allows the organization to see concisely and accurately the progress or regression. Fig 11.3 shows a comparison made over time.

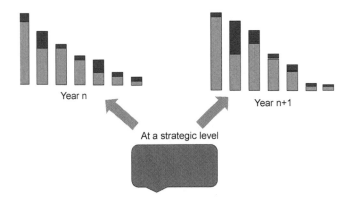

Figure 11.3 Are things getting better or worse?

## HOW TO IMPROVE THE CUSTOMER EXPERIENCE

Another really important strategic decision that can be made by looking at an analysis of the voice of the customer is where to put resources to improve the customer experience. Management never has unlimited resources. There is always contention for the resources the corporation has. And having the voice of the customer answers a really important question for management: "Where can I have the largest impact for the limited resources that I have to spend?"

In order to answer that really important question, management first looks at the high level summarization of the voice of the customer. Management finds the place where there is the most negative feedback. Management then isolates the negative comments for the category of data that is chosen. Management then "drills down" on the negative comments. The first step in the drill down process is to find what are the components of the topic that have had negative comments.

As an example, if the organization is a hotel chain and the topic of interest is product, then the components of product may be hotel, hotel room, shower, and balcony.

Once the components have been identified, the next step that is done is to identify the negative comments about each of the components. Suppose the component "bathroom" is selected. The negative comments about bathroom might include cleanliness, hot water, soap, towels, and mirror.

The drill down process from the high level categories all the way down to the specific comments about some components, gives management a roadmap as to how to dedicate resources for improvement of the customer experience. Fig 11.4 depicts the drill down process.

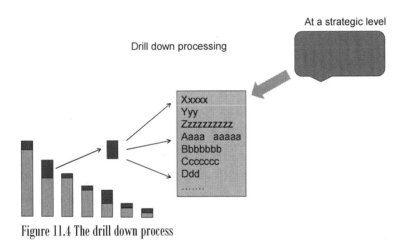

Figure 11.4 The drill down process

Fig 11.5 shows that once the component has been located, further drill down continues to show the cause of the negative feedback.

There is no question that listening to the voice of the customer has great strategic impact. But the voice of the customer can have great tactical impact as well.

The tactical impact is at the individual customer level. Whereas the collective voice of the customer is good for strategic decisions, the individual voice of the customer is good for immediate interactions with the customer.

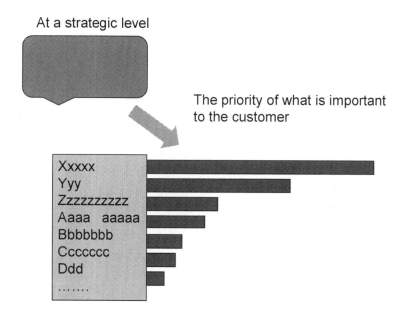

Figure 11.5 Further drill down continues to show the cause of the negative feedback

So where is individual contact with a customer made? The individual contact level with the customer is made via email, phone calls, and in face-to-face meetings.

And exactly how does hearing the voice of the customer manifest itself at the tactical level? The voice of the customer manifests itself in many ways. By hearing the voice of the customer at the tactical level, the company can prepare itself with:

- Scripts, leading to upselling and cross selling opportunities

- Prepared answers to questions that are likely to be asked

- Related offers

- Replies to complaints

Fig 11.6 shows how listening to the voice of the customer can be used tactically.

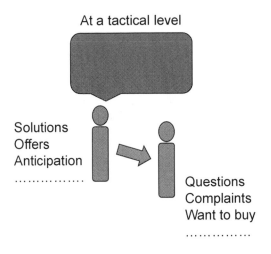

Figure 11.6 How listening to the voice of the customer can be used tactically

The real value of listening to the customer tactically is that the company can anticipate what the customer will be saying and can optimize the contact with the customer to turn the contact into a sales opportunity.

Whether strategically or tactically, the corporation puts itself into a position of becoming proactive in its individual marketplace.

## IN SUMMARY

There are two ways that a corporation can become aware of the voice of the customer: either strategically or tactically. When a corporation listens to the voice of the customer strategically, the corporation listens to the collective voice of the customer. When the corporation listens to the voice of the customer tactically, the corporation listens to the customer at the point of having contact with the individual customer.

Some of the ways the voice of the customer can be used strategically are:

- Setting a benchmark for grading the management of the company

- Determining what is important to the customer

- Looking at changes over time

- Finding a roadmap as to where resources should be used to improve the customer experience

Tactically hearing the voice of the customer can be used in many ways at the point of direct contact with the corporation.

# 12: Infrastructure

Visualizations are where the payoff is at in finding and analyzing the voice of the customer. Management uses visualizations to understand what is going on in the call center.

There is an irony however in the creation of the visualization. The irony is that the visualization is only the tip of the iceberg. In order to create the visualization, there is a whole infrastructure of work that has to be done first. 95% of the work is done before the visualization is done. The act of visualizing the data is only 5% of the work that is needed. Fig 12.1 shows this irony.

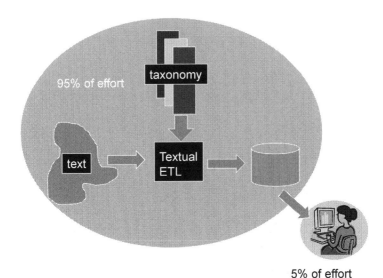

5% of effort

Figure 12.1 95% of the work is done before the visualization is done

## REFINING RAW DATA

The amount of work done after the database is created needs to include several other steps. In actuality, textual ETL only produces a raw content file. In order to prepare the raw content for analytical processing, a data refinement step is needed. Fig 12.2 shows this step.

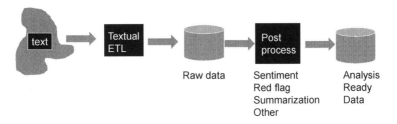

Figure 12.2 Refining raw data

There are several types of refinement that can be made. Some of the refinement processes include sentiment analysis, red flag analysis, summarization, and politeness analysis. After the refinement of the raw data content is done, then the data is ready for visualization.

## DIFFERENT KINDS OF VISUALIZATION

The visualization that is done is entirely dependent on the data being visualized and the technology used to do the visualization. Fig 12.3 depicts some of the kinds of visualization that can be done.

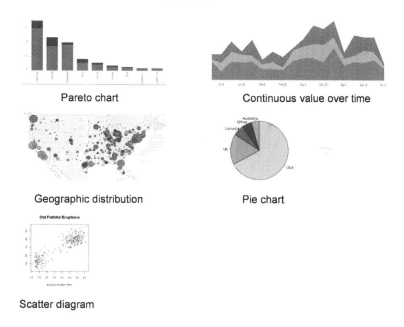

Figure 12.3 Various kinds of visualizations

Perhaps the most common form of visualization is the Pareto chart, also known as the bar chart. The bar chart depicts one or more values over time. Each bar represents a set of values as of a moment in time.

Another way to visualize data is by continuous value over time. This form of visualization is the same as the bar chart except that the data values are represented continuously.

In geographic distribution, different data values are represented by their location. The location can be global, the USA, Texas, or Dallas. There are many geographical distributions that can be used.

A pie chart shows the distribution of values except in the form of a pie. The pie chart is effective when there are not too many values to be represented.

The scatter diagram is used when many different measurements must be represented in a two dimensional form.

Some types of data lend themselves to one form of representation better than other forms of representation.

In the case of sentiment analysis, the bars do not represent data over time. Instead in sentiment analysis, the bars represent the supercategories of data – person, place, process, price, promotion, company, and product.

## ORIGINS OF DRILL DOWN PROCESSING

Most sentences have a subject and a predicate. And those types of words are regularly identified and used in the processing of textual ETL. Fig 12.4 shows some statements of sentiment and some predicates.

Figure 12.4 Sentiment and predicates

Predicates are normally part of a taxonomy. Fig 12.5 shows a taxonomy.

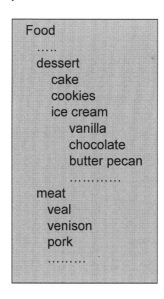

Figure 12.5 A taxonomy for predicates

The taxonomy seen in Fig 12.5 is an *n* level taxonomy. The hierarchical structure seen in the taxonomy contains the predicate. The predicate then can find its place in a larger hierarchy.

There are implications of this relationship between a predicate and its participation in a taxonomical hierarchy that are not obvious. Consider the analytical visualization drill down process shown on Fig 12.6.

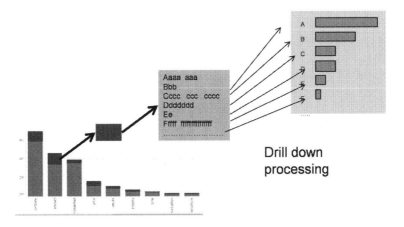

Figure 12.6 The analytical visualization drill down process

In Fig 12.6, the analysis starts with looking at the negative comments for a topic. The elements of that topic are displayed. Then the comments that relate to each of the elements are displayed. As an example of the drill down just described, the analysis begins with the topic product. Product has in it the elements hotel, hotel room, balcony, and reservations. Hotel room has in it bathroom, furniture, WiFi, television, and bed. When you look at the negative comments about bathroom you find hot water, mirror, soap, shampoo, and towels.

The analytical process has followed a hierarchical path. So where does that hierarchical path come from? The hierarchical path comes from the data that has been generated from the hierarchical taxonomy.

Fig 12.7 shows that the analytical drill down process can be tied directly to the hierarchical taxonomy that has been used to shape the data.

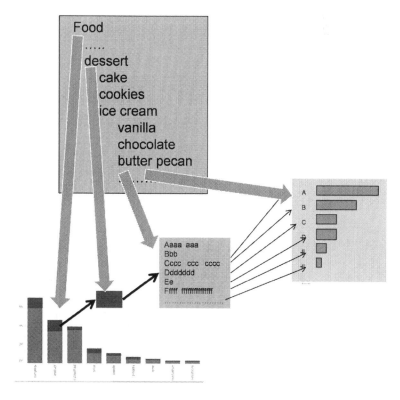

Figure 12.7 The analytical drill down process can be tied to the taxonomy

## UNIT OF TIME

One of the most important considerations in designing the data for the analytical database is to make sure that the unit of time over which the data is measured is appropriate to the data.

For example, measuring monthly sales by the second does not make any sense. Conversely measuring the changes in the Dow Jones Industrial average by the year is not terribly useful for most purposes.

When the data that is to be used for analytical purposes is designed, the unit of time over which the data is gathered and stored needs to be in synch with the data itself.

## IN SUMMARY

The creation of a visualization is the tail end of a long process. Textual ETL produces raw data. In order to prepare that raw data a secondary process.

The actual form of the visualization is quite varied. There are bar charts, continuous variable charts, pie charts, geographic chart, and scatter diagrams.

The ability to do drill down processing in analytical processing depends on the fact that the data being analyzed has come from a hierarchical presentation.

# 13: Combinations

There is great value in looking at the data that comes from text. However, that value is even greater when you use a combination of unstructured data and structured data. Fig 13.1 shows that databases whose origins are unstructured data and databases whose origins are structured data can be combined.

Figure 13.1 Unstructured and structured data can be combined

As an example of the value of combining unstructured data and structured data, consider the following. Once there was a restaurant chain that listened to their customer's feedback. One month they decided to count the number of complaints that came from each of their stores. At the end of the month they tallied the complaints and produced a simple bar graph. Fig 13.2 shows the bar graph that was produced.

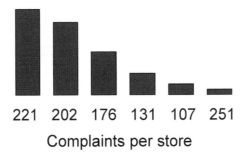

221  202  176  131  107  251

Complaints per store

Figure 13.2 Store 221 had the most number of complaints followed by Store 202

One could draw the conclusion that something was wrong with store 221 since they had the most complaints. However it turns out that store 221 is in Manhattan in Times Square. Store 202 is in the Chicago loop. Store 176 is in Monahans, Texas. Store 131 is in Castle Rock, Colorado. Store 107 is in Shreveport, Louisiana. And store 251 is in Las Cruces, New Mexico. The volume of business that passes through each store is vastly different. There may be more complaints in store 221 but store 221 has far more customers than other stores.

In order to get a better reading on the quality of the management in each store, a rating system is developed. The total number of complaints is divided into the total number of customers served. When this ratio is developed a very different picture is developed, as shown in Fig 13.3.

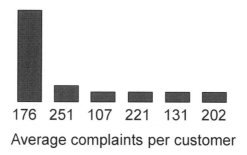

Average complaints per customer

Figure 13.3 Refined average of complaints

When the total number of customers per store (which is structured data) is divided into the total number of complaints, it is seen that the store in Monahans, Texas is much more poorly run than any other store.

The analysis using both data from the unstructured world coupled with data from the structured world provides a much more incisive analysis than data from just one world.

There is great value and great promise to bringing data together from both of these worlds. The question then becomes – how exactly does data from both worlds become combined?

The data from the unstructured world has no formal key structure. The information that goes into the database is whatever a person writes or says. There is very little (if any) formality of data found in the unstructured environment.

On the other hand, the data found in the structured environment is full of keys. Database designers and data administrators have spent their careers carefully organizing the data found in structured environment.

Because the data between the two environments is so different, it seems that trying to combine the data is very difficult. In order for data to be meaningfully combined from the two environments, there needs to be some intersection of data between the two environments.

Fortunately there is an intersection of at least some data that occurs in both environments. That data is:

- Money
- Time
- Geography

Fig 13.4 shows the intersection of data from the two environments.

It is fortunate that time, money, and geography is common among the two environments because those parameters are the very ones that are important in corporate decisions.

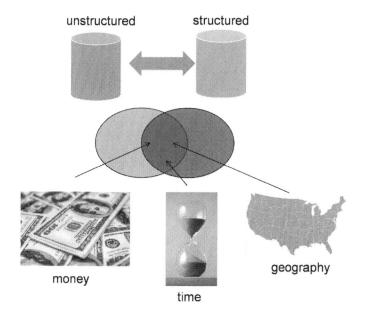

Figure 13.4 The intersection of data from the two environments

## IN SUMMARY

There is great analytical value in creating a database from textual data. There is even greater value in combining textual data and structured data.

In order to combine textual and structured data, there must be an intersection between the two environments. Fortunately there are some common areas between the two environments. These common areas include money, time, and geography.

# Index

Made in the USA
Middletown, DE
18 January 2020